THE GIRLS' GUIDE to Growing Up GREAT

SOPHIE ELKAN

with **LAURA CHAISTY** and
DR MADDY PODICHETTY

Illustrated by
Flo Perry

GREEN TREE
Bloomsbury Publishing Plc
50 Bedford Square, London, WC1B 3DP, UK

BLOOMSBURY, GREEN TREE and the Green Tree logo are trademarks of
Bloomsbury Publishing Plc

First published in Great Britain 2018
This edition published 2020

A catalogue record for this book is available from the British Library

Library of Congress Cataloguing-in-Publication data has been applied for

ISBN: PB: 978-1-4729-7358-0; eBook: 978-1-4729-4375-0

4 6 8 10 9 7 5 3

Designed and Typeset in Amasis by Anita Mangan
Printed and bound in Great Britain by CPI Group (UK) Ltd. Croydon, CR0 4YY

MIX
Paper from
responsible sources
FSC® C020471

To find out more about our authors and books visit
www.bloomsbury.com and sign up for our newsletters

THE GIRLS' GUIDE to Growing Up GREAT

SOPHIE ELKAN

with **LAURA CHAISTY** and
DR MADDY PODICHETTY

GREEN TREE
LONDON • OXFORD • NEW YORK • NEW DELHI • SYDNEY

Dedicated to all you girls
and to all the women
you'll become

CONTENTS ♥

WELCOME! (AND A BIT ABOUT US)

Hello! Welcome, and how are you?

It feels a bit weird, not knowing who I'm talking to – you might be in Year 5 or 6, or perhaps you're all the way up in Year 8 or beyond. Either way, you're here and that's great!

You might be wondering a bit about who we are. So here goes…

I'm Sophie and I've got a lovely girl of my own who is about your age.

Sophie

For my job I write – mainly magazines and the odd blog. I work part-time and mostly at home, sitting at my kitchen table with a big mug of tea. I really like it when my daughter brings her mates home after school, and it has been wonderful watching them grow up. What is less wonderful is when they get into muddles and shenanigans and fallings-out. Last summer there were a lot of fallings-out and it felt like every week her teacher was saying, 'Oh, the hormones kick in at this time, and it all goes a bit crazy.' So I thought I should get my daughter a book, something she could read on her own or pick up every now and then to read any bits that seemed relevant. When I looked I couldn't find one that I thought I might have wanted to read when I was her age. They were either a bit 'teachery' with way too much information in certain parts, or they were just a bit too girly and daft. You might have heard that 'knowledge is power' and when I thought about what I would have wanted to read I realised, 'Oh! I could write that book myself'. So here we are.

There are all sorts of things going on in your brain when you're growing up. Things that can feel quite far removed from the sort of thing you may hear in school about hormones and pituitary glands. As well as having some medical info, I thought it would be helpful to have an equally expert level of advice from a trained psychotherapist (someone who helps people going through emotional problems). My fabulous sister-in-law, Laura, has been a therapist for 19 years, so I didn't have to look too far to find the perfect person.

Laura

She says, 'I wanted to contribute to this book because I have a lot of experience dealing with the difficulties people can face when they bottle up their feelings. Mental health problems have a big impact on many aspects of life – from self-confidence through to making and managing relationships and how we make our way in the world. I am interested in how you look after your emotional health and in helping you find ways to get the support you may need as you go through the changes you face during puberty.'

As it happened, a new doctor had joined our Health Centre and she seemed pretty cool. I asked if she'd like to write the medical bits of this book.

As she herself says, 'Obviously, as well as being a doctor, I'm a person, too! I remember what it was like to be younger, and think that no grown-up could possibly understand what I was thinking or feeling, but please hear this: doctors see *everything*. So, if you have worries or need a bit of reassurance about how you're developing and you can't face asking someone in your family, or your school, please think about asking your doctor because that's what we are here for. We will try to make it as easy as possible for you, and I can tell you – we do not embarrass easily!' Well that makes sense, doesn't it?

By coincidence all three of us are mothers to girls and share an interest in how they get to grow up with self-confidence, self-belief and a strong sense of their identity. The idea of writing something together, with each of us talking about what we think is helpful, sounded like a good plan.

I wanted the book to have loads of illustrations, and it was really important to me that they should be interesting to look at, funny, sweet and also representative of all the great girls out there. When I saw the sort of thing Flo Perry was creating I crossed all my fingers and toes that she might agree to work with us and – hurrah – she did!

Each section will have me talking for a bit, and Maddy or Laura (or both of them) will add their advice, or offer some facts that may be helpful or interesting. But, it's not about us, is it? That's why we've included comments from girls your age – they're in speech bubbles throughout the book and look like this ⬤ and also some words of wisdom and experience from girls in their late teens or early 20s all the way up to some 70-year-old ladies who (and this may surprise you) felt *exactly like you do now* when they were younger. Their comments look like this 👓. The point is that they got through it and so will you!

Read the book all in one go, or dip in and out of the bits that seem relevant when you fancy it. We've also left some spaces in the book for you to doodle in the blanks, so let your imagination take you to some wild places and add your own notes – this is *your* book, just like it's *your* body and *your* brain – go for it and make it your own! Start by drawing your own portrait here, if you like.

It's a funny thing, growing up. One minute you're all there in the playground, boys and girls mixed up. Some of the boys are being a bit boring and playing together, some of the girls are huddled up in little groups having clubs or very important things to discuss, but essentially there's a load of you playing Tag or Jail, or something where you all get to run around a bit. The next thing you know, Tag has changed to Kiss Chase, some of your mates are suddenly acting a bit weird, and you're getting a bit moody but you just don't know why. Boys have either suddenly become a whole heap more interesting or a whole heap more annoying (or maybe a bit of both!). And your friends? The ones

you've been knocking around with since forever? Well, this could be a time of massive changes if you're in Year 6 and preparing to go to a new school, or you could already be well into secondary school and your old friends maybe don't fit so well into your life any more. Perhaps you're even having different sorts of feelings for girls and you're not sure what that might mean – are you LGBTQ*? What does that even mean anyway?

GIRLS CAN'T WHAT?

It might also be that you're hearing some stuff about what girls can do, and what boys can do. So, before we get started, here's some of the things girls can do:

GAME FOR HOURS ON END

RIDE A BIKE   THROW   RUN

KICK A BALL

LOVE PARKOUR   DRIVE A BUS

FLY TO THE MOON

WRITE A SCI-FI BOOK

BECOME AN ENGINEER OR AN ARCHITECT

BE THE BEST AT MATHS

---

*LGBTQ - lesbian, gay, bi, transgender, queer

Are you getting the point? Basically, girls can do EVERYTHING that boys can do and if they want to they can also:

PLAY AROUND WITH MAKE-UP

TRY MAD THINGS
WITH THEIR HAIR

STYLE OUT
THEIR CLOTHES

TALK TO EACH OTHER ABOUT
HOW THINGS MAKE THEM FEEL

CRY, AND GET A CUDDLE (AT ANY AGE!)

I'm not saying boys can't do any of these, but if they do, it can make them stand out a bit. If you know any boys who do these things, that's cool, because they aren't afraid of being different.

This is the ONE THING that boys can do that girls can't:

WEE STANDING UP

Sorry – just can't be done (without getting very messy).

Part 1
YOUR BODY

DIFFERENT STARTING PLACES

As you grow older, your body starts changing. The general term for this is 'going through puberty'. It marks the official start of adolescence, which lasts from the beginning of puberty up to adulthood. If you're reading this book you might have already started, or think you are about to. The 'average' age is 10–13, but it can even happen earlier than that. 'Early puberty' can affect girls from the age of seven. It's also not unusual for these changes to happen much later – you may be 15, 16 or even older. This is not because of anything you might have done, and there is nothing you can do to make puberty start sooner or later. Your body becomes the boss of you and these changes will start happening when your body is ready.

MIND + BODY = YOU

It can be quite a strange feeling, when your body takes over. You think it's your head that decides what you do and what you like – it's your head that tells you that you like ham and pineapple on your pizza and you can't stand mushrooms, right? But guess what? Your head and your body have been secretly working together all this time. Right now, it may feel as if your body has taken control and is acting on its own. If you have a better idea of what's actually going on, it will really help your head and body work together, and that is much more reassuring than imagining those two bits that make up the you-ness of you working against each other.

So, where are you? Are you one of the older girls in your class or one of the younger ones? Are you taller than the boys? Are you shorter than most of your pals? Are you a bit chunkier, or a bit skinnier, or kind of in the middle? Is your skin dark, pale or somewhere in the middle? Do you use legs, or are you on wheels? Do you get bad hay fever, asthma or eczema? Have you got loads of freckles? Have you got a scar that can tell a tale, or several scars or even birthmarks and you worry that they define you? Which ethnic group do you identify with? Maybe you wear glasses, maybe you don't.

We all start from different places, and we all have our own unique personalities and characters. We don't all like the same things, and just because you might now wear a crop top for PE doesn't mean you don't also still enjoy going mad on a trampoline.

The simple truth is when you start puberty you'll go through it your way, but it's a pretty similar deal for everyone. There will be changes taking place that you can see, and some that you can't. On top of the periods, hair, spots – all the stuff you've probably heard about – there'll be a lot going on in your brain, too, and that can sometimes feel a bit harder to deal with.

DR. MADDY

We are born with all the hormones that make the changes during puberty already in our bodies. Hormones are like chemical messages that your brain sends out to different bits of you. But, they are not active until the body has grown and developed enough for the time to be right. That is why puberty can start at different times for all of us.

Puberty starts when hormones are released from the brain. The **hypothalamus** ('hi-pah-tha-la-muss') section of the brain (which is roughly behind the eyes) controls things like thirst, hunger, sleep and mood. It is responsible for triggering the **pituitary** ('pit-u-it-tree') gland (another part of the brain). The hormones from the pituitary gland kick-start the production of specific female sex hormones, oestrogen ('east-ra-jen') and **progesterone** ('pro-jest-er-own'). **Oestrogen** starts off breast development as well as changes in your vagina, your uterus (or womb) and also your Fallopian tubes or oviducts (the bits that carry eggs to the womb). Progesterone also controls your menstrual cycle (periods). You can find more on this on page 39.

Hypothalamus

Brain

Pituitary gland

These aren't the only bits of you that may change during puberty, though. Here's a checklist of things to expect as you start maturing, and moving on through the next few years. They may happen in roughly this order but not necessarily, so don't worry if some are happening, but not others:

Puberty checklist

✦ Your breasts will start to grow.

✦ You'll notice pubic hair (short, thick, curly hair) growing around your genitals.

✦ Your body will get taller and bigger. You'll start to shoot up in height, and may also start noticing your breasts becoming fuller, and your hips and thighs becoming curvier.

✦ You will start having periods, also known as monthly bleeds (because they usually happen once a month).

✦ You'll probably get some spots on your face.

✦ You will notice that your body smell starts to change. Everyone (kids and adults) gets pongy feet but the rest of you starts to get a bit sweatier, too.

✦ Hair will grow in your armpits and other hair on your body or face may get darker or more noticeable.

✦ The hormones racing around your body also have an impact on your brain, so your feelings may seem larger than life and a bit harder to figure out.

✦ You might find yourself being attracted to people in a different way. Instead of thinking someone seems like they'd be a nice friend, you may start fancying them.

⇨ DIFFERENT STARTING PLACES ⇦

BREASTS

Breasts, boobs, baps, bosoms – there are a lot of words to describe your chest as a woman, and no matter what you call them, the ones you have are unique to you. When puberty starts kicking in, your breasts are one of the first things to change.

This is what a lot of people think that 'normal' breasts will look like once they are fully grown:

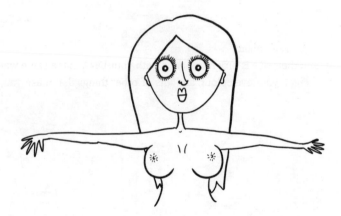

However, there are as many different 'types' of boobs as there are 'types' of most things – think about it, say your best friend has blue eyes, are they the exact same colour blue as every blue-eyed person on this planet? Are they blue like the sky? Or more blue like your favourite jeans? The thing you'll find out as you and your friends start to develop is that there isn't really a 'normal'. Every one of us is *just a little bit different*.

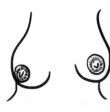

Breasts can be huge, tiny (sometimes barely noticeable even when they're fully grown) or somewhere in between. They can start off a bit pointy, sort of cone-shaped, and some will stay like that. Others will keep growing and becoming fuller and rounder. It's worth mentioning that sometimes one will grow at a faster rate than the other. You could well have different sizes on your chest for a while, but the smaller one should catch up eventually. That said, quite often adult women's breasts can be slightly different sizes, which may sound a little freaky but think about it – it's true for most women out there, and how often have you noticed it? The point is, each of us is different and there's nothing you can do to make your breasts bigger or smaller. Your boobs are your

boobs, and their size is programmed in with your DNA in the same way as your height, your eye colour, and lots of other things that make you, you.

CROP TOPS AND BRAS

Once your breasts start growing, make sure you get properly fitted for a bra, especially for when you do sports – breasts are full of delicate tissue, and they need a bit of support if you're going to be bouncing around. If they've only just started changing, you could think about getting a few crop top vests to wear under your clothes. Crop tops are a good first move as the more fitted fabric and style will help hold everything in and give some support, even if you're not quite ready for a bra (or don't want to be the only girl in your class wearing one). If your breasts get bigger you will need to move on to an actual bra. You might have seen a few different styles around. Some are really simple, some are pretty fancy with lace and twinkly bits. The main difference is whether or not a bra has wire underneath the front section (underwired), which gives the whole thing more support. Eventually, if you have bigger breasts, the underwire option may be better for you but at first a simple bra will be fine. You might like to have one with a pretty design or bright colours, or you might prefer something plainer – that's up to you. The only thing you need to do is make sure it is the right size for you and that it is comfortable and it is supporting you properly.

Perhaps you've had a nosey around the underwear section already, or even bought one or two bras. Hopefully you have one that fits well and does its job – which is to support your breasts. A good-fitting bra shouldn't feel uncomfortable at any time. Other than feeling supported, you shouldn't be aware that you're wearing one. If you take your bra off at the end of the day (you wouldn't sleep in a bra) and it's left a red mark anywhere it could be that it needs a bit of adjustment (you can fiddle with the straps to make them longer or shorter) or it may mean that it's no longer fitting you properly and you should think about going to get fitted by a pro.

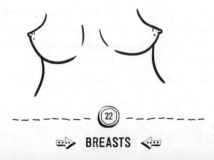

Getting fitted for a bra

Bras are sold in a vast number of sizes, and these can seem a little overwhelming when you're taking your first steps into 'Bra world'. All bra sizes have a number and a letter (e.g. 28A, 32AA, 34B). The number part is the measurement in old-fashioned inches, not centimetres, across your chest where the bra fastens, and the letter bit is the cup size (the cups are the bits of fabric that hold your breasts in place). The higher the letter in the alphabet, the bigger the boob, basically. So a D boob is bigger than an A.

The fitters are all women. You'll go into a cubicle with one of them, whip your top off and they'll measure you across your chest with a tape-measure. They are extremely experienced and have seen breasts of every size, shape and age and if you don't feel comfortable with the idea of taking your clothes off just wear a fitted crop top or vest. Then they'll get some bras for you to try on and can wait outside the cubicle while you do this if you prefer, but don't be shy to ask for help if you need it. They'll check the fit of the bra once it's on and make sure your breasts are 'sitting' properly in the cups.

It's really important to find a bra that fits you properly, and that means going for a fitting. This really isn't a big deal and won't cost you a penny. What's more, having a fitting doesn't mean you have to buy a bra there and then or that you owe it to the shop to get the one they suggest. It's just the most accurate way of knowing which size you should be wearing. Most department stores (M&S, Debenhams, etc.) have a fitting service and there are also a few shops on the high street that specifically sell underwear (or lingerie as it's more fancily known – pronounced 'lon-je-ray').

ABOUT NIPPLES

Nipples can be any colour, from pale pink to rosy red; milky-coffee coloured through to dark brown. They also vary hugely in shape – some women have small nipples, others have large ones. Pretty much, though, they're all round and made up of two bits: the nipple itself (the pointy bit that can stick out) and the areola, which is the circle of coloured skin around the nipple. Some people are all about the nipple bit, with little areolas; some are more the other way. The areola can sometimes have little raised bumps on it – again, normal!

Nipples are where a baby will get milk from, when feeding from the breast. They tend to be about a third of the way up from the base of the breast, but can be lower. They will usually stick out a bit as they are super-sensitive, and can often seem as if they have a mind of their own. Lots of things can cause them to get hard – particularly if you're cold,

or if you're excited about something. Some, however, never pop out to say hello. These are called 'inverted' nipples and they're not unusual. You may hear people saying they're something to worry about but honestly, they're not. If they start out as 'innies' (inverted) then that is simply the way you're made. Have a feel of your breasts as they grow. It can feel nice touching them, and that's a good thing! Don't be afraid to have a squeeze.

A lot of things can feel as if you have no control over them during puberty – you're just starting to get used to your body changing – but remember, it is still your body. Own it!

LAURA ON: BREASTS

The prospect of being the first girl in class to wear a bra might feel really scary, but equally being the last girl to need a bra can be worrying too – you may feel like you are never going to start changing alongside your friends. Everyone around you might be buying pretty bras or showing off their new crop tops and it can make you feel worried, sad and even frightened that something is wrong. It isn't. You are you and you will grow at the rate that is just right for your body. And, it's not necessarily those girls who are into make-up and boys who will start to grow first; it could be the sporty girl, or the girl who's really quiet – it could be anyone!

The fact is we are all surrounded by images and pictures of 'ideal' women – from slinky fashion models to music videos featuring women with big boobs in clingy clothes or even pictures where $\longrightarrow$

women aren't wearing anything on top at all. Sometimes our breasts can feel like they are public property but they're not. Your breasts are just yours, and having big or small boobs doesn't need to define anything about your personality or how attractive you are.

DR. MADDY

Let's look at the structure of breasts and how they grow. The breast area is exactly the same in boys and girls before puberty. The changes in your breasts are controlled by your female hormones.

The diagram below shows your breast area before and after the changes brought on by puberty:

Ducts or tubes

Nipple

Ducts growing

Breast tissue develops

Buds or glands form for milk production

Tissue grows

These changes come about because the brain is sending messages (releasing hormones) that tell your body that it's ready to start developing.

The brain sends hormones through the bloodstream to the ovaries

Your nipples will start to stick out more and might change colour. Underneath your nipples might feel slightly tender and a bit harder when you feel them – these are your breast 'buds' growing and they will slowly get bigger to form discs of breast material under your skin. The nerve endings in your breasts make them sensitive to being touched. It can feel nice and at those times your nipples might become harder and stand out.

BREASTS AND PERIODS

It is very common for your breasts to feel fuller and more tender or sensitive just before a period, too, but this usually eases after your period has started each month. There are things that you can do to help with this tenderness, such as wearing a supportive bra and eating fewer salty things. That might sound a bit random but because of the hormone activity in your body around your period, your body tends to hold on to more water (known as **water retention**) and this might make your breasts a little swollen. Reducing your salt intake can help the body to process the amount of water it really needs. If it gets really bad, ask an adult if you could have some paracetamol – this could help. (And do always check with a grown-up before taking ANY medication.)

FLAT CHESTS

Sometimes a girl's breasts will look as if there has been no change with puberty, and they remain flat. It could be that the nipples have grown or swollen, or even that there is a small amount of softer tissue around the nipple, but not enough to need the support of a bra. When you have clothes on, it might look as if there has been no change. If this sounds like you, don't worry. It doesn't mean that your body hasn't gone through or won't go through the other hormonal changes – you will still get pubic hair and your periods will come regardless. It's just that it can take a bit of time for breasts to grow, so they may develop in time or not, but remember: each of us is different – from watermelons to fried eggs – there really is no 'normal' when it comes to size.

You could doodle your boobs onto one of these blank figures, and then use the other one to imagine what your boobs may be like when they've finished growing.

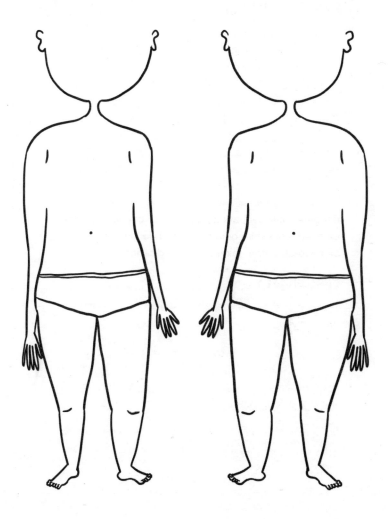

LAURA'S Q & A

"Since my breasts started to grow my best friend has been acting weird around me. She keeps saying that I've changed and it's really bugging me."

The thing is, you are changing, but if you are developing at a different rate from your friend she might be concerned that you'll leave her behind, and worry that things will alter in your friendship. Change can be tricky for everyone to get used to, not just the person it's happening to.

Your breasts growing can make you feel pretty unsettled. You might notice yourself becoming tearful or angry and sometimes really sad and it's difficult to know why. You might take things to heart that wouldn't have bothered you before. Though your body is ready to make all these changes, you might not feel emotionally ready and might even wish it wasn't happening. So, it might not just be your friend who is struggling with these changes in you.

Talk to your friend, let her know how you're feeling. This way you can share your concerns without one or other of you assuming you know what the other one is thinking. Friends sometimes need some help to know what's going on!

Try to make sure the two of you have some fun stuff to do so that you keep remembering what you like about each other and can keep laughing together.

Names for your breasts

Here are some names for breasts that we were told by the girls your age – some are really funny! Add some more of your own if you like, however weird!

boobies	*buds*
boobs	*tits*
apples	*jugs*
bob and bill	
coconuts	
diamonds	

WHAT'S GOING ON DOWN THERE?

I'm going to start this section off with a confession. When I was younger, I thought that 'down there' were only two holes — one for wee, one for poo. I sort of assumed that all the baby-making and period stuff happened in the wee hole. You might already know more than I did, and know that women actually have three holes: one for wee, one for poo and another one for the baby-making and period stuff.

First things first. Although there are many, many words used, the official name for the outside bits of the pants area for both girls and boys is the genitals. For girls, the specific term is vulva. The vulva has the vaginal opening inside it, and it is the vagina that, when the time comes, is the baby and period area. The 'wee hole' is actually called your urethra. And the one for poo? That's your anus, which is the opening to your rectum (where the poo comes down). I know these words aren't exactly familiar, are they? We don't say them every day — they don't really pop up in conversation, so it can make you feel a bit self-conscious saying them. They're only words, though, and they are the correct terms, so don't feel funny about using them.

DR. MADDY

I want to say something about when you have health concerns involving your vagina (or your bottom). Because these parts aren't on public view (like our hands or legs are) it can feel like a big deal to show your bits to the doctor. Remember doctors have seen everything before and these are all just parts of your body.

SHORT AND CURLIES

Let's start with the vulva. This is the bit from just above that little slit between your thighs, all the way down to the vaginal opening between your legs. Just above that crease is a softer, raised area, perhaps a little bit padded, and this is your *mons pubis* or pubic mound. It's here where you may first notice pubic hair growing, when the time comes. Pubic hair is hair that grows between your legs once you've started puberty. Unlike the hair on your head, it's usually a lot shorter, and is often (but not always) pretty curly. Everyone, girls and boys, grows pubic hair during puberty. It is thickest around your genitals, where it forms an upside-down triangle shape, but can start as a line growing down from your belly button. It can get quite thick and bushy, or be a little sparse. Our 'pubes' (slang for pubic hair) are normally hidden in our knickers but imagine if we got a little bit creative down there...

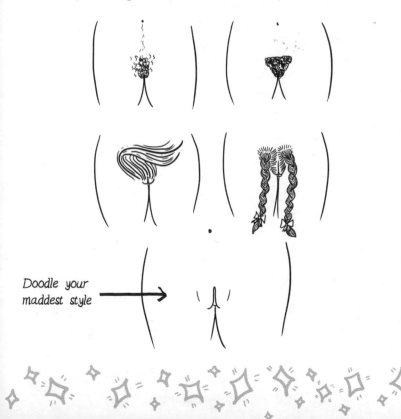

Doodle your maddest style →

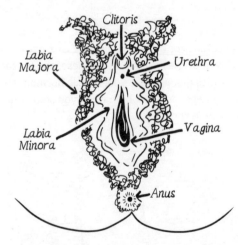

AND NOW FOR THE SCIENCE BIT

Next up we have the labia majora and minora. Labia is a Latin word, meaning lips, but these are more like folds of skin. The majora are the bigger folds but there are also smaller folds (minora) directly around the vaginal opening. These aren't always identical in size and shape — you can have one that's bigger than the other and this is absolutely normal. Nothing to worry about. Their job is to protect the opening because the vagina goes all the way up inside you to your uterus (womb). It is in your uterus that babies can grow and when you have your period this is where the blood will come out. Last, but not least, there is the clitoris, which is like a little bud that is found just at the top of labia majora, under the pubic mound.

Clitoris

Labia Majora

Urethra

Labia Minora

Vagina

Anus

While boys' bits are all on the outside, with girls most of the action is happening in areas that are harder to see. Use a hand mirror (e.g. a make-up or compact mirror) to have a good look and get to know yourself. It's also a great idea to have a bit of an explore with your hands/fingers. Make sure you've given them a wash, so you're not spreading any muck that may be lurking under your fingernails, and have a feel of yourself. It might be a bit strange if you're not used to it but, remember, it is your body. Get to know it! Obviously, this is something you'd do in private but it doesn't have to be all dramatic and secretive. There's a big difference between secretive and private. Secretive has a bit of a sneaky sound to it, doesn't it? Whereas private – that's just something that is your business and up to you alone as to who else can know about it.

Your whole genital area is super-sensitive (again, this applies to boys, too). You'll notice different textures – some parts are a bit smoother, some a bit squishier, some even a bit rougher or more bobbly. What you'll probably notice is that your clitoris is hyper-sensitive to being touched. It can be quite a weird feeling, but in a good way – this pea-shaped button is supposed to feel nice when you touch it.

Your outside bits connect with your internal genital organs: the vagina leads to the uterus (as already mentioned) and leading from your uterus are your Fallopian tubes or oviducts (there are two, one each side of the uterus) and your ovaries (again, two of these, one for each Fallopian tube). It is the ovaries that produce your female hormones and also release an ovum, or egg, once a month when you start your periods. (More on this in the next chapter).

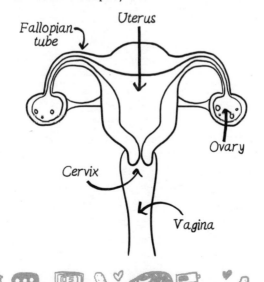

DR. MADDY Q&A

"*I'm really scared and worried because I think there is something wrong with me. I've got what looks like a scraggy bit of skin hanging down just between my legs on one side of my vagina, and I've never seen anything like that before.*"

The first thing to say is please don't worry! It's perfectly normal. As Sophie says, our labia are often different – different sizes from each other, so a bit uneven, and certainly different from our friends or family.

Vaginas are like all body parts – the ones we have are different to anyone else's. No two are the same. Some of us have larger labia minora, and they can stick out a bit – either on both sides of the opening, or sometimes just on one.

LAURA'S Q & A

"I'm the only one of my friends to have hair growing down below and it's making me feel really self-conscious. I feel like I can't go swimming or go to sleepovers because I'm worried they'll laugh at me."

As you probably know, starting to grow hair is another sign that your hormones are active. I understand it can be unsettling to see your body changing. You might not like the feeling that you're not in control. Your friends will be growing and changing too – even if they are not growing hair it may be that their breasts are starting to grow, or they're getting the odd spot. I'll bet that all of you are feeling quite self-conscious and not wanting each other to notice any signs of difference or change. I also reckon that they will be so busy keeping the attention away from their body changes that they won't really be focusing on you and be bothered by what's going on with your body.

Could you imagine talking to one of your friends about this? It could be a good idea, even if that might sound like an embarrassing conversation to have. You might be reassured to hear that they, too, are going through some other change and could do with a good friend to talk to. I don't mean it has to be an intense and serious chat – you could end up laughing with each other.

Remember, there is nothing freaky about growing hair, it is a sign that everything is working well and you are developing. We all find it a little strange when things change. It takes us human beings a while to get used to new experiences!

It's a funny thing, but a lot of girls and women won't refer to their vagina as … well … their vagina. Often your parents will give it a name and talk about your 'twinkle' or your 'fairy' (?!). Of course it's up to you what you call the parts of your body – calling your legs your 'pins' or your nose your 'schnoz'. There does seem to be something about vaginas though that invites some curious nicknames. Here are a few that I heard from the girls I interviewed – have you come across any?

Names for your vagina

Add some more of your own if you like, however random!

nunu	foof
vajayjay	fanny
privates	vanjang
fufu	
front bottom	
downstairs area	
bits	
flower	

PERIODS

Ah, periods. They really do seem to define puberty, don't they? There is *so* much emphasis on them and so much chatter and gossip – who's started? Who hasn't? Someone's sister who started during PE, someone's mum who told all her friends on Facebook, that girl further up the school who has to go and lie down in the nurse's office every month. And those odd, alarming words – leaks, aches, tampons, towels, spotting, cramps, cycles. Is it really blood? Why is it brownish? It goes on and on.

> *I was so excited to start my period and the excitement hasn't worn off yet! I was the last of all my friends to start and I felt really left out.*

First things first, Dr. Maddy is going to explain exactly what is going on.

DR. MADDY

A period is a monthly (or thereabouts) 'bleed' from your vagina. It usually lasts between three and seven days, although it can be longer or shorter.

Your first period marks the start of your menstrual cycle: when you have your first 'bleed' (period) is called menstruation, and it's called a cycle because it's a sequence of events that repeat (they go round and round) – you'll get your period roughly every 28 days.

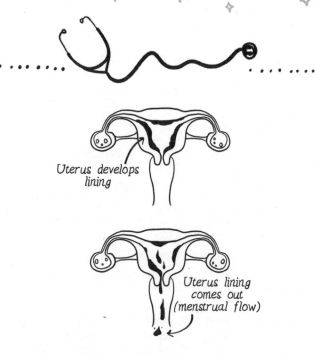

Uterus develops
lining

Uterus lining
comes out
(menstrual flow)

All women are born with millions of tiny eggs already in their ovaries. Our ovaries are connected to our wombs, and it is in our wombs that babies grow (not our tummies!).

Your periods start when the hormones in your brain 'tell' your ovaries to start releasing these eggs into your womb or uterus (same thing, different names). Each month one of these eggs will be released from the ovary and travel down the Fallopian tube to the womb. To make a baby, this egg will need to be fertilised by sperm. If an egg is not fertilised then it will travel through the womb, or uterus, down the vagina and out of your body with the menstrual fluid.

Your uterus prepares each month for this egg by creating a thick, soft lining for itself. If the egg isn't fertilised then this lining isn't needed and it is broken down into a fluid, which we call menstrual fluid or blood, which also travels down through the vagina. Menstrual fluid is not really blood, like when you cut your finger, and you'll notice it is more brown or maroon in colour, but people describe it as blood and talk about 'bleeding' during their periods. Around three to five tablespoons of liquid come out during an average period – not that much really, but it takes between three and eight days for the whole process to run its course.

The average woman starts a new menstrual cycle (has a period) about every 28 days, but not everyone is the same. I should also say that for some of us our periods can be very irregular and not follow that monthly pattern. There may be some months when you don't bleed, and others when there isn't a full 28 days between cycles – you might have a period twice in one month. The medical term for this is **amenorrhea** ('am-en-or-rear'). This should settle after a year or two and doesn't mean there is anything wrong. You will have periods until you're around 50 years old. The time when your periods stop is called the menopause.

You won't know exactly the moment when your period is going to start, but your body is giving you hints. It could be that your breasts will start feeling a bit sore, you'll have a few more spots than usual, or will feel a bit of cramping.

Another indication that your period might be on its way is that you may feel a bit sticky between your legs, or even notice a yellow-whitish stain in your pants. This slightly gooey substance is called discharge and comes from your vagina. It is a sign that things are working as they should be, and is is healthy and normal. Also, once you've started your periods you might be aware of this discharge a couple of weeks before your period starts each month.

MASTER YOUR PERIOD

If you are getting signs about once a month, your periods are probably going to start soon. You might notice spots of blood in your knickers for a few months before your periods actually start. Not a lot, but just the odd bit now and again. This is called spotting and is another

My period was pretty much what I expected apart from the blood's a lot browner than you'd think!

common sign that your periods are on their way. It's a very good idea to try and get to know your body and its workings, and so it's well worth keeping a note of when you're getting these hints (like in your diary or on your phone if you have one, or you could download an app – check for one with decent ratings. You should start to see a pattern.)

You might also get a little sign about two weeks before your period starts, when the egg is released from the ovary (mid-cycle). This is called the *mittelschmerz* – 'mi-tel-shhmertz' – it's a nice word, isn't it? It's German and means 'middle pain'. Not everyone gets it, but if you do you may notice that it coincides with a bit of discharge. It's all part of getting to know your body and your individual cycle. Even if your cycle isn't 100 per cent regular, if you're tuned in to the signs that your period is coming it will help you be prepared.

If you think your period is due you can make sure you have some pads or tampons in your school bag so you're good to go once it does. More on these on page 45.

Even if you're prepared for your period, I bet you're still having mixed feelings about it. You can doodle in the picture below how it feels for you, or how you imagine it will feel – is it like a river building up, a popping balloon, a spiky cactus?

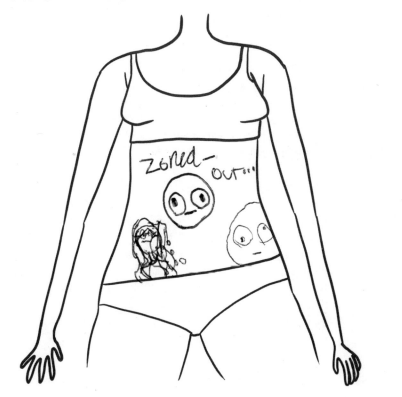

DEALING WITH LEAKS

Your period shouldn't stop you going about your day-to-day activities just as normal. That said, being on your period is a time when you should be having a full daily body wash. When your body is busier than normal it makes sense to keep it in tip-top condition.

If you're keeping track of your cycle you should have a good idea of when your period is due and hopefully avoid leaks or spills. It's inevitable, though, that every now and then you'll be caught short and a bit of blood will go on your clothes (knickers mainly) or perhaps your bed sheets. If this happens, don't panic – we've all been there. The wonders of science are helpful to know at this stage – basically, use cold water to 'dilute' blood, and get the colour out of material. Don't use hot water because it will 'fix' the blood and make a permanent stain more likely. If you do bleed on your knickers, whip 'em off (when you can!) and soak them in cold water for 10–15 minutes. Once you're done (as best as you can), wring them out and leave them to dry before putting them in the laundry bin. If it's over your sheets, again cold water is your friend – dab it over the mark, or if it's bigger than a mere dab-sized area take the sheet off your bed, soak the whole thing in cold water and then wash as normal. You may end up with some knickers that are a little stained, even after a soak and washing: these can be kept back for next month – every female in the land has a pair or two of period pants in her underwear drawer!

PADS, TOWELS AND LINERS

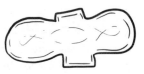

Lots of girls use pads (also called sanitary towels) during their period. You can buy them in different sizes – 'maxi' ones for the first few days when your blood flow is heavier, and smaller ones, or panty liners, for the last few days when the flow becomes much lighter. You might also want to use panty liners if you're getting a bit of discharge before starting your period.

All pads have a sticky back so they can be fixed into your pants which can be a bit less fiddly than using tampons. Some have what are called 'wings'. Don't get too excited – they don't hover over your knickers! The wings are side flaps which help to keep them firmly in place. Pads absorb the blood once it has left your vagina. These need to be changed frequently during your period (every 3–4 hours). Larger pads for night time are also available to buy.

Years ago, pads used to be really thick and weren't always comfortable to wear (in fact, way back when, they didn't even have sticky backs; you had to fix them with hooks to a sort of belt around your waist). These days they're thinner, more absorbant and much nicer to use. They even come in a little plastic pouch for you to wrap up your used pad before you stick it in a bin. Do remember you should NEVER flush pads, liners or tampons down the loo. Our toilet systems just can't cope and you could block up the loo, never mind wreaking havoc on the environment. Check with your mum or dad if there is a particular bin in the house for used pads and tampons. If you're out and about and using a public loo, you've probably already noticed special bins in the ladies' loo. These are specifically for pads and tampons.

You can also buy reusable, washable period pants – search them up online. They have different levels of absorbencies so you should find some that suit you and your cycle. They are certainly better for the planet.

USING A TAMPON

It might be a good idea to start off with pads while you're getting used to having periods and then if you want to, you can try using tampons. A tampon is a bit like a cotton plug – you put it inside your vagina so that the blood doesn't come out. Like pads, you can buy tampons in different sizes for different times of your period (bigger for the heavier days, smaller for the lighter ones). There is a string on the base that you pull to remove them before putting a fresh one in. Do make sure you always remember to take the old one out before you put a new one in – that's really important. It can be a good idea to change your tampon when sitting on the loo – that way you have good access to your vagina and can fiddle around more easily. Oh, and by the way, if you're wearing a tampon you needn't worry about going for a wee – the tampon won't come out unless you pull on that bit of string so don't fret that it could fall out without your knowing.

At first, tampons can seem a bit more fiddly to use. Like pads, you need to change them regularly (it's a good idea to use pads at night-time when you're asleep as it's really important to change tampons at least every eight hours). Some tampons come with applicators that help push them into place; some you can just insert using your fingers.

The applicators are cardboard or plastic tubes, and tampons with applicators will be in a larger packet. Neither is better than the other – you just need to figure out which works well for you. If you do find the applicator style easier, please remember that the applicator bits (cardboard or plastic) should also never be flushed down the loo – they'll need to go in the bin too.

When you first see a tampon it will look tiny and you might wonder how on earth it will ever absorb all the blood that seems to come out during your period. That's because tampons grow bigger once you've popped them in. Get a glass of water and stick a tampon in to see what happens. It grows as it absorbs the liquid and this is just what it will do when it is inside you. Tampons need to be changed regularly, just like pads.

TOXIC SHOCK SYNDROME

The other reason you need to change tampons often is because there is a (very rare) infection you can get if you keep a tampon in your body for too long. It is called Toxic Shock Syndrome (TSS). It is extremely unlikely that using a tampon will cause TSS but it is a very serious infection and so you do need to be aware of it. The symptoms can include a high temperature, feeling dizzy, faint or sick, diarrhoea, and a rash on your skin. If you think you may have these symptoms, take the tampon out and see a doctor or a nurse as soon as possible.

Whatever form of protection you use, do remember to wash your hands thoroughly before and after, especially if you're using an internal method (i.e. putting something inside you).

I haven't started but sometimes I have bad cramps.

If you're having a few signs that your period is on its way, go to a chemist or a supermarket – even your corner shop – and have a browse around the 'Feminine Hygiene' section. You'll see loads of different types of products. Some are more eco-friendly, some have a scented smell, and there are different pack sizes and different levels of absorbency for different

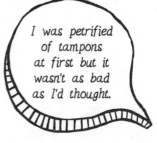

I was petrified of tampons at first but it wasn't as bad as I'd thought.

times during your period. Have a look and get to know what's on offer.

BE PREPARED

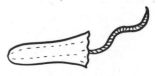

Don't try using a tampon before your period actually comes as it's not a good idea to put one in if you're not actually menstruating. Perhaps start off with a packet of pads, which you can practise using so you'll be ready when you need them. It's a really good idea to have a couple of pads and a spare pair of knickers in your bag if you think your period might be coming. Stick them in your school bag or have them to hand if you're at a mate's house. Don't stress about it but being prepared is never a bad thing. If you don't have anything with you and you're at school when your period comes, ask a teacher or the school nurse. If you're really stuck you could wad up some loo roll and pop that in your knickers until you can get hold of a tampon or a pad. And most ladies' loos (public and school) will have machines selling tampons and pads – see if you can spot the machines next time you're nipping to the loo.

If you're feeling cramps or other symptoms in your body, or your emotions feel a bit out of control (or all of the above!), and it's happening on a monthly basis just before your period actually starts, then you have something called premenstrual syndrome (PMS). Years ago it was known as PMT (T for tension) and some people still call it by that name. Many, many girls and women experience this.

'I was nine years old, two months after my birthday. I bled into my Minnie Mouse knickers and tried to shove them in the washing without anyone seeing.'

'I was 15. I had to get my dad to buy me pads as mum was out. Cringe!'

FEELING A BIT ROUGH?

You might have heard older girls or women talking about cramps or period pains. The muscles your uterus is using to get rid of the menstrual fluid – the lining of the uterus – aren't used every day so it's only natural that they'll feel a bit sore when they're called into action! If the cramps are bad, try having a warm bath or using a heat pad or hot water bottle on your tummy, or do some stretching to try and ease the aches away. Any of these things can feel soothing.

It might seem as if you just want to crawl into bed but quite often you'll actually feel better if you can keep active – it gets your body working and could help to keep your mind busy. Run around to work off some of those sluggish feelings; even a stroll can be relaxing. The fresh air will pep you up a bit, and if you go with family or a friend the chatter will help take your mind off what's going on inside.

WORK OUT TO WORK YOUR HORMONES

As well as puberty hormones, your body creates other hormones, or chemical messages released by the brain, at different times and sparked off by other things. **Endorphins** are hormones that you can trigger through exercise and laughter. Endorphins are those happy feelings. That whoosh of great feeling you get after working up a sweat? Endorphins. That relaxing goodwill you feel after you've been giggling non-stop for hours with your friends? Endorphins, my friend.

If you can get up and get active when you have your period or are struggling with PMS, your body will give you a natural reward by releasing endorphins and they can act as a natural form of pain relief. So, if you're feeling like you're glued to the sofa and all you can think about is your period, try getting up, getting out and working up a sweat. Getting in the pool can be a great idea if you feel comfortable wearing a tampon. You can still do PE – feel smug afterwards when your brain lets out a burst of endorphins. Failing that, get some friends together to get you laughing.

'I was 16 and I was the last girl in my class to get my periods. My mother fixed me up with a pad and my father was waiting for me in the car because we were all going out. My mother followed me to the car, obviously thinking she should inform my dad, but she couldn't find the words. She said, "J is er ... unwell." My father replied firmly, but not angrily, "I never want to hear you say that again. She is not unwell; it is a natural healthy thing. Are you alright love?"'

LAURA'S Q & A

"I get really down just before I have my period. Is this normal and will I grow out of it?"

I can't say if this is something that you'll experience in the long term because these things tend to change as you get older and your periods settle into more regular rhythms. Some women really notice symptoms of premenstrual syndrome and others less so, but just because you feel it now doesn't mean you always will. Having your period is a natural and healthy thing, but it can make you feel under the weather, even if you're not actually ill. During this time, you might feel more sensitive to things people say, and more affected by stuff happening around you. You could be trying to ignore how you are feeling or telling yourself to snap out of it. Don't be hard on yourself. Lots of people are often really good at being kind to friends or family but can sometimes be tough on themselves. Imagine a friend was telling you that they're having a tough time – I think you'd be really supportive and tell her to look after herself. I wonder if you can give yourself a bit of this kindness?

Try keeping a diary of your experiences – you might start to notice patterns developing that could help you try and plan around your periods. If you know that you'll be feeling really pooped, try not to plan full-on events; if you know that you start feeling snappy with family, make a plan to go to the cinema with some friends. If your friends drive you batty when you're on your period, suggest a Saturday sofa night with your family. If you find you really crave chocolate (or some other treaty thing) then go easy on the treats for a bit before your period is due so you can enjoy them when you want them most.

On a practical level, come up with some ideas to boost your mood when you have your period. Think of those things that feel like giving yourself a big hug: curling up in bed for a bit, having a soak in the bath, or cuddling up with a hot water bottle (or your favourite teddy).

This probably won't make the down feelings disappear but it might be a way of getting through what is usually the first few days of your cycle.

Why not write your own ideas down here as a handy reminder?

. . . .

. . . .

. . . .

. . . .

. . . .

. . . .

LAURA'S Q & A

"Everyone in my class has started their periods apart from me. I have told them that I've started too, but I'm worried they'll find out I'm lying."

It sounds like you're really worried that you're not in the same place as everyone else (assuming of course that they are all telling the truth and that others aren't also feeling under pressure to lie). There is nothing wrong with starting your periods later than your friends. Your body is doing exactly what is right and taking the time it needs to get you ready for this step, but I know it can be hard to feel left out.

Saying something that isn't true can be a real burden because you're worried that you'll be found out and might be scared of the effect on your friendships. At some point, all of us have told a story to make ourselves look and feel better – you won't be the first or last girl to say she has started her period when she hasn't because it's natural to want to fit in.

The thing to remember is your body is private and you don't have to talk about the changes going on with anyone else if you don't want to. Your periods will come and you can be confident that your body knows what it is doing.

Words for 'periods' we've discovered during our research

Some of these are well known, some not so much. Add any you've heard below!

monthlies	*Aunt Bessie*
Auntie Flo	*code red*
coming on	*the reds*
time of the month	*the curse*
menstruation	
having the painters and decorators in	
bloody hell	
codename 'pyramid'	
lady days	

LOOKING AFTER YOUR BODY: SPOTS, HAIR, SWEAT & SHAPE

You might not have thought too much about your body while you've been busy growing up. It could be that you've always been self-conscious about your ears sticking out a bit, or the fact that you've got a birthmark on your chest. Maybe you've always been a bit chubby, or everyone calls you the string bean and tries to feed you up. You might, of course, have thought a lot about your body if there is something about it that is different from others. The way your body changes during puberty, however, is slightly different.

While you are going through puberty there is a surge of hormones that are racing around adapting your body for adulthood. These are the things that cause the changes. Some affect all of us: spots, sweat, hair growth, changing shapes. Girls will get periods, boys will develop an Adam's apple (the lumpy bit halfway down the front of their necks) and their voices will get lower, but all of us – all of you – will go through some changes.

YOU'LL DO IT YOUR WAY

Although this is common to everyone, you will change in your own way. It may be very different from the way in which it happened for your sister, your friends, your cousins – basically any other girls you know – and because of this you might end up feeling like you're the only person going through this. You're not. Honestly. Even if you feel that you're the one who has that embarrassing spot on your chin that is so big everyone must be looking at it, you should know that the chances are that everyone in your class will be feeling a bit self-conscious for some reason or another – the girl with massive boobs will think everyone's staring at her, the girl with a flat chest will think people are whispering behind her back. Ease up on yourself and remember you are a whole person. You're not just a spot, or a breast, or a knobbly knee. In fact:

YOU ARE NOT JUST THE BODY YOU WALK AROUND IN

You are a heart and a mind and a good friend, and a great sense of humour. You're smart and maybe a bit cheeky, or perhaps you're quite quiet and your friends know they can depend on you when they need someone to chat with. Maybe you're not so good at English or Maths but are great at inventing things, or design or sport. Just because there are changes going on, these things don't change.

It's not like you'll wake up one morning to find your face covered in spots, your shape completely changed, your armpits bushy with hair, and when you raise your arm to look further a big whiff of BO (body odour) is going to spring out.

Things happen gradually, in their turn.

SPOTS

Getting spots is maybe the most visible sign of your body going through changes, and spots can appear a year or so before your period starts. I know it's tempting to pick them (believe me!) but please, do bear in mind that your skin can scar and this is the time in your life when it is so important to take care of yourself. Remember – it is YOUR body. As well as meaning it is yours to enjoy, yours to decide how you want to look and how you want it to work, it also means it is your responsibility to *look after it*. Of course it's annoying when some well-meaning adult tells you not to pick at your spots but listen, if you ignore them it isn't really going to affect that interfering adult, is it? It's going to affect you. So, you may want to start taking a little more care of your skin, and getting into some habits that will benefit you for a lifetime.

GOOD PRACTICE FOR YOUR SKIN

First things first: it helps to keep your skin clean – getting spots is due to hormones but if you don't keep your face clean it can make the whole thing a lot worse. Use a gentle cleanser/soap and water to clean your skin morning and night – different products work in different ways so I'm not going to give directions here. Browse around the shops for something simple and basic that you like the look of and you'll find instructions on the pack. You really, truly don't need to be getting anything too fancy or too expensive. I'm also a big fan of moisturiser – again, just something light and gentle. You're not an old lady, and you don't need a rich, heavy cream suffocating your young and – apart from a few spots – fresh skin. Getting into the habit of moisturising is a good thing when you are washing your face more often – it can help if your skin feels a little tight after washing. You might not think you need any more oily stuff on your face because your spots are oily enough, but it's a different sort of oil and even the spottiest skin can dry out.

If you *have* to squeeze a spot, make sure there's no grime on your fingers – even lurking under your fingernails. If you have a squeeze but nothing's happening, leave it alone. It's not ready to pop and if you force it that's when the scarring could happen. If you develop acne – which is when you have more than a few spots now and then – you can go and see a pharmacist or a GP who may be able to prescribe something that will help. Spots can really get you down so don't be fearful about asking for help. (And look around – you really aren't the only one suffering).

When we talk about getting spots, these fall into two types: blackheads and whiteheads or pustules. During puberty the pores of your skin (teeny holes that help the skin to breathe) start to become larger, plus your skin's oil glands (sebaceous glands), release more oil (sebum) around your body, specifically on your face but possibly also your back, chest and shoulders. This sebum isn't in itself a bad thing but the whole thing can go into overdrive, causing spots to form. Blackheads are pores that have become blocked up by sebum, a bit like a plug. The top bit that you can see becomes darker, hence the name blackhead! Whiteheads are the same sort of thing – a blocked pore – but there is skin over the top, so they don't show up as black. They can become inflamed and have pus or fluid in them. They can also be red around the edges and a bit sore.

Most spots don't have to be a big deal – if you have lots of spots and particularly if they are sore, it may be that they can be treated by a pharmacist or by your doctor, so don't suffer in silence.

HAIR

As well as pubic hair growing on your genitals, you'll also find that you grow hair under your arms and the hair on your legs (and face) may get darker and more noticeable. There are also other places where you may find an increase in hair activity. All humans – boys and girls – are covered in hair. It's all over (in fact everywhere apart from the palms of your hands and the soles of your feet). Your genitals, legs and armpits are the most common places, but it is normal to notice it in other places – arms, face, nipples, bum, back – you name it.

I'd love to say 'Hey! Go with it, we all have body hair and why should society tell us to get rid of it?', but life is a bit more complicated than that, isn't it? You might not want to have hairy legs or you could feel self-conscious wearing a vest if you're the first to start growing armpit hair. It's not helped by the fact that most of the images that surround us show very hairless women. In fact, it's really rare to see a famous woman with armpit or leg hair but that is because they remove it – it's not because that hair isn't growing.

DR. MADDY

Pubic hair is different to the hair on your head. Quite often it's curlier, even if your head hair is straight. This is because its 'job' is different. The coarser, springier texture is due to its role as an added layer of protection. This makes sense as your groin is generally more delicate than your head. Pubic hair can also be a different colour – often closer to the colour of your eyebrows.

HAIR, THERE AND EVERYWHERE

Hair growth is certainly nothing to be ashamed of. We come in all different shapes and sizes and some people are just hairier than others. A lot of women choose to get rid of some of this hair, others are happy to leave it. If you're fair-haired it may be less obvious, but if your hair is darker than your skin it will probably show up more. You may find as you get older and feel a little less self-conscious talking about these sorts of things that you and your friends will share stories about teenage years spent trying to remove bits of your body hair – each of you thinking you'd die if anyone knew you had hair on your legs, under your arms or even a bit of a moustache (even though, of course, we all do). It's a shame that it is only when we get older that we are able to share these things. I'm not suggesting you should tell all your friends if you find a random hair growing out of your cheek or sprouting out of your nipples, but please do know that you won't be the only one.

LAURA'S Q & A

"Everyone in my class has smooth legs but my mum won't let me get rid of the hair on mine. It makes me feel really self-conscious and also like the odd one out."

I can see you are in a difficult position between your friends and their expectations, and your mum and her ideas of what is right for you. From what you've said I'm not sure what you want to do – whether you want to get rid of the hair on your legs or just want to get rid of the horrible feeling of being the odd one out.

When friends start to do a new thing it can feel like you must join in, but the problem with this is that it doesn't give you the chance to make up your own mind – and making decisions about your body is really important and will continue throughout your life. There is a lot of pressure put on girls to fit in with particular views of what is feminine, and there are not many positive images of women with body hair. This is really sad but says more about how women are portrayed in images we are given through the internet, social media, and on television, than it does about how women really live.

I wonder if you could find some time to talk to your mum and explain to her how hard it is to be on the outside of your friendship group. Your mum might be trying to let you know that you don't have to do what everyone else is doing but she may be missing that you feel caught between wanting to fit in and not wanting to fight with her.

SWEAT

As well as new hair growing, another thing that you may notice is that you are sweating more. All over your body sweat glands – three million of them! – have been activated by puberty, and they start producing a different type of sweat in a load of new places.

The trouble with sweat really starts when it gets a bit whiffy. While your body is going through puberty even fresh sweat can start to pong. You may be conscious of a bit of a waft coming from your armpits and lots of people think that this is because of the hair growing there, but hair in itself won't make your pits start to get smelly. Armpits that have had the hair removed will still whiff if there's been some heavy duty sweating and no washing. It's not just your armpits, either. You need to make sure you're washing at least hands, feet, armpits and groin each day as these are all the places where sweat likes to linger. And you'll probably notice your hair is getting greasier (lank and clumpy) more quickly and you might have to up the amount of washes per week. Jump in the shower before school or have a bath at night – however you like to do it – to make sure you're keeping clean on a daily basis.

As well as needing to wash yourself more often, you may need to wash your clothes more frequently – especially your underwear, which needs to be clean on every day. Do everyone a favour, and figure out how to use the washing machine for yourself! It's not hard, I promise. Most clothes can be put in for a 30-degree wash and some machines have special cycles for trainers and other sports shoes, so there's no need to bin them when they start to pong – just bung them in the machine and give them a day or so to dry out.

DR. MADDY

We all sweat, but as your body goes through puberty you will start to sweat more due to the increase in your sweat glands. Humans have two types of sweat glands: eccrine sweat glands and apocrine sweat glands.

Eccrine glands are responsible for the 'fresh' sweat that the body produces to cool itself down if the weather's warm or you have been active – this is light, water-based sweat that on its own won't cause any odour. Before puberty this is the only type of sweat your body produces and so it is unusual for your body to 'smell' of sweat (unless you're not clean, of course). Sweat is actually a really important bodily function. It helps your body maintain an even temperature and when you get too hot the body gets busy efficiently producing sweat to cool you down.

Apocrine sweat glands are activated during puberty and give off a different type of sweat, which can create an odour when it is released by the gland and is sitting on the skin. Our apocrine sweat glands are mainly located in our armpits, our groin and our bottoms. This sweat isn't caused by being hot or running around a lot, but is instead connected with our emotions – stress, excitement, etc. Therefore, it's important to keep clean and fresh all the time – not just on summery days or when you're doing sports.

LOOKING AFTER YOUR BODY: SPOTS, HAIR, SWEAT & SHAPE

WHAT TO USE

You can use an anti-perspirant deodorant daily, and this will help stop the sweating. Unlike a straightforward deodorant, which masks the sweat smell with a fragrance of its own, anti-perspirants help reduce the amount of sweat produced. You'll see it is sold in a few different forms – the most common are roll-ons, sprays and sticks. They all get used directly on your armpits, and it's up to you which you get on best with. Roll-ons and sticks can take a few more seconds to dry, but equally, spray can get up your nose a bit.

It's worth having a look next time you're at the shops. As with all of these things, you don't have to rush to get everything at once, and you may not find the right one for you first time around. Although all that choice can be dazzling, it also means you can try out different things and find out what works for you. Some products – anti-perspirants, shower gels, soaps, bath gels – can have very heavy fragrances and may not be suitable for your skin type, especially if you're prone to eczema. Again, try things out and if you do get any sort of reaction (redness or rashes) then move on to something else.

LAURA'S Q & A

"There's a girl in my class who smells really bad and people laugh at her behind her back. This makes me feel really uncomfortable, but it's not like she's my friend so I'm not sure whether or not I should get involved."

There's quite a bit going on here, isn't there? You are obviously concerned about this girl, which says good things about you. You've noticed something that you feel is exposing this girl to harsh treatment (the way she smells) and this is relatively easy to fix. You could have a quiet word with a grown-up who knows her (like a teaching assistant or the class teacher) and let them know that others are laughing behind her back. You don't have to give masses of details – just say you're worried, and ask for their help. I think it would make you feel better if you knew you'd done something about this but it isn't your job to actually fix this for her.

It might be that there's something else that's worrying you about this, so I want to share something with you – there was a girl in my class at school who looked pretty neglected and sometimes really smelled. Like you, I felt bad for her and didn't know what to do. Looking back, I think I was worried that the others would think if I spoke up for her then I was her friend and that could mean I was left out like she was. When I think about that as an adult I suspect that I was afraid of being judged and rejected by my friends. It can be an intense time for friendships. Check out the chapter on Friends IRL (In Real Life) on page 99 for more on this.

SHAPE

Both boys and girls change shape during puberty. Girls may see their upper arms, hips and thighs getting fuller, while the waist narrows and becomes more defined. You may not be aware of these changes taking place – they could be very slight. Or, you could find your shape changing quite a bit if you're destined for bigger breasts and/or curvier hips. Whether it is very noticeable for you or barely noticeable at all, it's a healthy part of the process. You may or may not put a bit of weight on during this stage and it could be that just the idea of this feels like an absolutely massive deal. Please try and remember, this is about your body changing into an older, adult you.

Sketch out your changing shape in the mirrors below:

Me at seven   Me now

'I was quite disappointed my boobs weren't growing as fast as my friends'. They never did catch up!'

'I didn't really realise my body was changing too much as it was quite gradual.'

'I was a bit scared but also excited when my body started changing. There's a lot of pressure from other girls to grow up fast. If you start your period later or your boobs don't come at the same time as everyone else, it can feel like you're being left behind since that's all they ever talk about.'

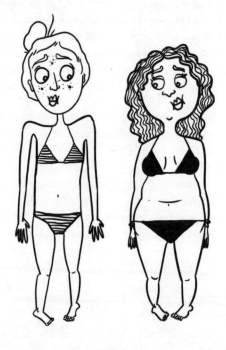

LAURA'S Q & A

"People keep making comments about my body. It's making me feel really self-conscious and I don't like it."

Even though we all go through puberty, some people have clearly forgotten what it feels like and can be insensitive to how you may feel. I'm guessing that the last thing you want at this time is someone drawing attention to you in a public way.

Remember, though, that this is your body. Growing up and changing is nothing to feel uncomfortable or embarrassed about. You can't stop people making comments but if they are bothering you it doesn't hurt to speak out and tell them to mind their own business. Think up a polite but firm way of telling them to butt out! Your body is changing because you are growing up, and part of growing up is learning to speak out about the things that bother you in a way that those around you will hear and hopefully respect.

You might also be feeling self-conscious because you yourself are feeling a little unsure of the changes taking place. It can take a bit of getting used to, but the important thing is for you to feel happy in yourself. Have a good look at your body both dressed and naked so that you can get used to your shape. Wear clothes that make you feel upbeat and comfortable as you develop a relationship with your changing self. Get to know and celebrate your body and all that it can do so that you feel confident about the developing you.

DR. MADDY

During puberty, your body goes through a massive growth spurt – you'll reach your adult height during these years. It might be that you seem a little chunkier than usual and then this is followed by a growth spurt so, as you get taller, you return to your usual shape. Also, your trunk or torso (the main bit of your body minus your head and your arms and legs) is usually playing catch up as growth tends to start off in your limbs (arms and legs).This can mean that your tummy, chest and back can seem to be carrying more weight, but once this area catches up with your limbs it stops being so noticeable.

There's also a lot going on under your skin, including a hormone spurt, and this can lead to an increase in your appetite – you may find yourself getting hungry more often, and wanting to eat more than previously. We gain weight when we eat more calories (the energy units by which food is measured) than we burn off during activity. If you're spending a lot of time online or in front of the telly but your body is telling you it is hungry all the time you may well put some weight on. There's a difference between a changing shape and weight gain. Try and make sure you find the right balance between what you eat and how active you are.

There's a whole bit in the chapter on Periods about the benefits of exercise on your mind (see page 50) and

of course, it also helps your body to grow strong and
healthy. If you don't think of yourself as sporty or if PE
lessons don't interest you, remember that getting active
isn't just about lessons. You may be into dancing or
gymnastics or perhaps you feel amazing after an energetic
tennis lesson or love that feeling you get after a long walk
in the fresh air. Try out new things and when you find the
one that works for you, enjoy it.

Your changing shape shouldn't be an excuse to hit the biscuit tin and
not come out for four years – that would be daft. Neither is it about
calculating every mouthful in a bid to keep yourself thin. Whatever
your natural shape, we all need to eat, and eat healthily to help our
bodies grow. Of course, everyone fancies a treat from time to time, and
that's not bad or wrong. Going out for pizza with your friends should
be one of life's joys, not something to worry about, and having some
chocolate or a bag of crisps now and then is OK. However, when you're
having a treat, make sure you enjoy it or what's the point?

Food isn't 'good' or 'bad' – it's necessary for our survival. It really
is about balance. If you're getting your vitamins, protein and fibre
through lots of veggies, fruit, nuts, meat, fish, potatoes, rice, pasta and
bread, that's great. Keep fried stuff like chips for once or twice a week.
These are the basic rules. Be really wary of new popular diets (such as
fasting – not eating – some days, or restricting what you eat to just a
few types of food), and take with a pinch of salt anyone suggesting you
should not eat a certain food group like carbs (carbohydrates) or fats.
All food groups are *necessary* for good health – they each play a part in
a balanced diet. Yes, some people may have allergies or intolerances
but they are surprisingly few. If you think you may have an allergy or

an intolerance, get yourself tested by your doctor; don't just cut certain foods out of your diet. Get into cooking and enjoy food (I guarantee whoever usually does the cooking in your house will love the help!). It's that thing again about this being your body and it being your responsibility to look after it.

FAT AND THIN

It's also worth saying that it's not food as such that makes you fat or thin: it's how much and what you're eating. When people say stuff like 'Oooh, chocolate is bad', what they mean is it is more fattening than some other foods (like lettuce!). This is because it has higher amounts of fats and sugar so if you eat it for breakfast, lunch and dinner you will put on a lot of weight.

If you're carrying extra weight this is thought of as being a bad thing, not just something that might mean you're not as healthy as you should be. I hear a lot of stuff about how terribly, awfully bad it is to be fat, and I hear fat used as an insult or a way of describing someone who is lazy or unable to control themselves. Fatties are often the baddies in stories and films.

It's as daft as thinking that all thin people are really fit and healthy – or even that they're a bit miserable and are so busy being thin they have no time for life's pleasures. No one wants people judging their bodies, and being described as gawky or 'skin and bones' is hurtful – there are no two ways about it. We all come in *different* shapes and sizes and all of us have something about our body that makes us unique. You just need to make sure you're healthy and fit, both of which are possible, regardless of size. This stage in your life is about figuring out who you are and that is so much more than being a certain weight.

LAURA ON: FOOD & FEELINGS

Sometimes eating becomes tangled up with our emotions. Yes, we eat to get the energy needed to keep ourselves going, but food is about pleasure as well as nutrition. We all have things that we like and dislike (as with most areas of our lives). I personally love cauliflower but my children think it is horrid, farty food – just like I did when I was their age!

Our taste changes as we grow, but what we like and don't like can sometimes become a battleground in the family. Arguments around food can spark up easily, particularly if you feel very strongly that no one cares what you personally do or don't like eating. For example, if you are a vegetarian and the rest of your family are not, you may feel like no one understands or supports you. Talking about this calmly out of the 'argument zone' and coming up with compromises (where you get a bit of your way, and your parents get a bit of theirs) can be really helpful in taking some of the tension out of these situations. Also, as Sophie says, getting into the kitchen yourself and taking on some of the responsibility of preparing the food you are eating can be a great way to take the heat out of those battles around the dinner table.

Another way in which our relationships with food can become more complicated is when we see food as a way of managing our moods. I'm sure we all have memories of being given certain foods to feel better when we've been upset, or as a reward when we've done something to be proud of ('if you're a good girl we'll have chips for supper', or 'you can't have pudding until you've finished your veggies'). Or it could be that in your mind you might associate a particular food with a particular time – soup when you're ill, ice cream on holiday, family pizza night – and your memories (good and bad!) of those times get muddled up with your feelings about the food you've eaten. You might want to recreate one of those feelings – especially if you're feeling low.

It actually makes sense that food, feelings and behaviour can get tangled up. If you think about it, feelings are often experienced in our stomachs. We talk about having 'gut feelings' or 'butterflies in my tummy' in certain situations when our emotions are stirred up. It's easy to see why our relationship with food is more complicated than simply seeing it as fuel to keep our bodies going.

In some cases eating can become a really big problem. When eating too little or too much starts to cause health problems, it might be diagnosed as an eating disorder. There are three main types of eating disorders: anorexia; bulimia; and compulsive over-eating. **Anorexia** is when a person severely limits what they eat and/or does too much exercise to ensure they do not put on weight. Of the three, it is probably the most dangerous to your body as losing weight and fat can have serious consequences. It can be very hard for people who have anorexia to change their eating habits as the main cause might really be how they feel about their lives, not just their bodies. **Bulimia** is when someone eats loads of food (binges) and then gets it out of their body before the food is digested. Similarly, **compulsive over-eating** puts strain on the body and this can lead to long-term problems. What all three have in common is that people with these conditions are really suffering in their bodies and also in their minds. Just being told to change doesn't work and expert help is needed.

If you are stopping yourself having the food you want, or feeling like you must be constantly on a diet, or if you find it hard to stop yourself eating even when you know you've had enough, it could be that your own relationship with food has tipped off balance a little. If so, it is important to talk to someone you trust about this, as you could need help. Getting into unhealthy eating habits is not good. Usually there is something emotional going on underneath and talking about this and thinking it through with someone else can help you make sense of what's really going on and help get your eating back into balance.

NICE FEELINGS

Your body has a trillion nerve endings in it and these create feelings that can give you physical pleasure – sinking into a soft bed, the breeze on your skin when you've worked up a sweat, rolling down a grassy slope. You get the idea. Sometimes those lovely feelings are brought about by someone else – a kiss goodnight, a lovely cuddle. And sometimes you can make them happen all by yourself. The fact is, there are bits of your body that will feel particularly nice when you touch them. That's how they've been designed.

Your nipples will have those sorts of sensations, and so will your clitoris. There are other bits, too, that might feel nice to touch – everyone is different. Boys often like touching their willies, and touching yourself because it feels good is really natural for both boys and girls. This is called masturbation or masturbating. For some reason, the fact that girls enjoy this as much as boys isn't spoken about much. Boys might chat about it with each other – maybe even showing off a bit. Girls, less so. I think it's all seen as a bit secretive – and remember how I said secretive can feel sneaky? It shouldn't be secretive, but it is a private thing. Touching and getting to know yourself in this way is perfectly normal.

Women and sexuality

There is a long history of research into how people think about sexuality and how men and women experience it differently. The thing is, until quite recently this research was mainly written by men, so probably can't truthfully reflect what women were really thinking and experiencing (and let's face it, as women have only been allowed to vote and own property for the last 100 years, men and women were a long way from being treated equally). There was social pressure on women not to speak about pleasure in sex and so a myth grew that women didn't like sex or enjoy masturbation. Nonsense! Hopefully these ancient ideas are finally being challenged by fabulous young women like you who know that masturbation can feel good and is a normal part of learning about yourself and getting to know your body.

LAURA'S Q & A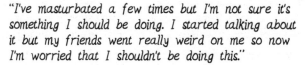

"I've masturbated a few times but I'm not sure it's something I should be doing. I started talking about it but my friends went really weird on me so now I'm worried that I shouldn't be doing this."

You're not at all weird for enjoying the feeling when you touch yourself, but because your friends didn't want to have a conversation about it, you're worried you are different from them. Believe me, the chances are your friends will be exploring their bodies, too, and experimenting with masturbation – even if they aren't admitting it. It's a funny thing that a lot of boys feel quite free to discuss masturbation with each other, but it tends to be something that goes undiscussed in groups of girls. That doesn't mean you shouldn't do it or enjoy it.

I do understand that it can be uncomfortable to be the person who speaks out about the thing everyone else might be thinking. I'm also sure that if your friends feel as awkward as they seemed to, they will quickly move on from the memory of the conversation. If they do keep reminding you it might be a sign that they want to talk more and also have questions about the subject. If they are real friends they will appreciate you for your honesty and not want you to feel uncomfortable or left out. It's not that you shouldn't talk about sex and masturbation with your friends, but you might find you come up against some embarrassment because it is a personal thing. Lots of adults struggle to talk about these subjects – even to their own children. Oh, and watch out for people saying stuff like 'It will make you go blind', or even that it will make you ill. These things aren't true.

AM I PRETTY?

OK, are you ready? I'm going to go against the 'Mother Code' here. The Mother Code dictates that when your daughter (or your son) asks, 'Am I pretty?' You have to say, 'Yes, of course, but looks don't matter, it's about who you are.' I don't think that's quite true.

Of course, who you are as a person is the most important thing and no matter what you look like, who you are inside is what will shine out. But ... I think looks do matter, although maybe not in the way that you might think, because we are all judged on appearances in one way or another. That can mean being judged on whether you are pretty, but it can also mean being judged on whether or not you look friendly, whether you come across as shy or outgoing. How we appear to others is only one aspect of ourselves but it is the one that we show to the world, and it is fair to assume it will be the first impression most people have of us.

We live in one country in a whole world made up of nearly 200 countries and what defines 'pretty' changes a fair bit if you travel across the globe. Some people in the UK use fake tan to make their skin darker, while in Korea people often try to be as pale as possible. And, in Fiji when it comes to body size, bigger is better. However, I'm not writing this book in Korea or Fiji, and in our country, regardless of race, 'pretty' usually means the following:

fabulous hair

long legs, a flat tummy and perky boobs

big eyes and long eyelashes

even skin tone – no blemishes!

Add some more ideas of your own!

. . . .

. . . .

. . . .

. . . .

. . . .

. . . .

. . . .

. . . .

. . . .

What do you think? It's quite a rigid list, isn't it? And, even if your look does by chance 'fit', I'm going to bet that when you look in the mirror you still might feel doubts about the face reflecting back at you. The thing about this list, though, is it doesn't even *begin* to cover all the things that we may be drawn to, or think are cool. Let's face it, if that's your list then the vast majority of us *aren't* 'pretty'. That's not to say that we're not beautiful, attractive, striking, cool, quirky, chic, stylish, amazing, remarkable and unique – all of which sound quite intriguing, don't they? Before you start to think about whether you fit the list, have a think about what you think of as pretty and how you yourself would like to look and what *you* think looks good.

I don't really know how I feel about how I look because people call me pretty and fit but other people call me ugly, fat and stuff.

I think I look kind and happy.

I like the muscles on my body.

Beauty through the ages

Our idea of what makes someone 'pretty' is very different now to what it would have been in the past – 50 years ago, what made a girl 'pretty' was not the same as 50 years before that. If you go right back to Tudor times ideas of beauty were totally different again – women like Queen Elizabeth I used to wear ruff-neck collars as they were on trend and shave their hairlines

back from their foreheads to make their faces longer – I know, right? That sounds disgusting to me (and probably to you, too) but back then it was thought to be essential if you wanted to be pretty. Fast-forward to the Georgians and their obsession with having the palest, whitest skin.

If a woman had a spot, or a scar, she would cover it up with a patch (or *mouche*). Fancy women would cut them out of black velvet and wear them like a beauty spot, but poorer women who wanted to look 'pretty' would use anything – apparently the skin of a dead mouse was quite a popular option (euuuggghh). Hop

forwards in time once more to last century and the 1950s, and Hollywood was filled with women who were much bigger than the celebrities of today. They were adored for their full figures – big boobs, big bums, strong legs. I know, I know, none of this really helps when you don't fit today's idea of pretty, but it's still worth pointing out. Close your eyes, imagine all these ideas of pretty – get a picture in your mind – and then open your eyes and look at yourself. It's a big world out there, made up from a long history and we are all just a tiny part of that. We don't need to be so narrow in judging ourselves.

Truth is, we are surrounded by images of 'pretty' and it's not so simple to find the 'beauty within' when all we see are pictures of girls who look kind of the same (and it's not like you). It may be that you want to look 'pretty', or perhaps you absolutely don't, but when all you see are these images, you can start to wonder if there's something wrong with you. If you don't look like these girls or women, are you different in some way? Are you not as good? Are you weird? Perhaps you don't want to look like them, but what does that say about you? Does that mean you're not normal? (And that's not to imply that 'weird', 'different' and 'not normal' are bad things!).

If you like having short hair, rather than long, does that mean you aren't girly? If you're bigger than those girls, does that mean you're not pretty? If you don't have big breasts are you still feminine? If you wear glasses does that mean your face isn't OK? It's so easy to start spinning out and questioning everything when something about you doesn't seem to fit with how the world expects you to be. Everywhere we look around us there are images of girls and women – billboards, magazines, telly, music videos, Instagram, Pinterest, YouTube, celebrities – that make it seem that girls should look a certain way. It can be really tough if that 'look' has nothing in common with you.

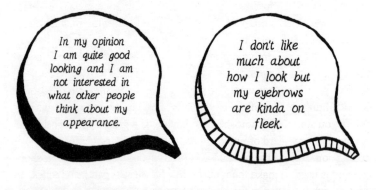

In my opinion I am quite good looking and I am not interested in what other people think about my appearance.

I don't like much about how I look but my eyebrows are kinda on fleek.

The thing is, a lot of these images aren't true to life. With those celebrities, whether they are on telly, in films, vlogs or music videos, or even just the ones who are massive on social media despite the fact they do nothing at all, it is THEIR JOB to look like they do. They don't just tootle around being gorgeous, they have teams of people they work with dressing them, doing their hair and make-up, taking their so-called 'selfies', telling them what to eat, and making them go to the gym at 6am every day (hard work!). They don't get to loll around in whatever they fancy wearing that day. They can't run to the park and have an ice cream just because the sun has come out after weeks of non-stop rain. And, if they ever do pop to the corner shop, there's always the risk that someone will take a photo of them looking less than their usual glamorous selves and it will be plastered all over the internet with people saying mean things.

Years ago, I worked for one of the biggest magazine publishers in the country, one that publishes loads of those glossy fashion magazines. When I started there, I worked as a booker (the person who arranges the photo shoots), which means I was the person responsible for 'calling in' models to see if they'd be right for the different magazines I was working on. We used to use loads of different models for the different magazines – older women for the magazines that have lots of cooking tips and health features, teenage girls for the younger magazines – and for the photo shoots that were for the high-profile fashion magazines, we had fashion models coming into the office on quite a regular basis. I'm going to let you into a not-very-secret secret: *they don't really look like they do in the pictures.* Not only were they caked in make-up for the photos, but clothes would be pinned to look like they fitted better. Good lighting can transform anyone's face and body, and all of this is before you start with Photoshop. Photoshop is a graphics editor that you might have heard of and it is used a lot in preparing photos for publication. Even if the model looks pretty fabulous before, Photoshop can and is used to make them absolutely flawless. It can trim inches from anywhere, it can make a spotty face smooth and glowing, get rid of bags under the eyes, it can change hair colour and make it longer or shorter — or even make sure there are no random bits sticking up where you don't want them!

BEFORE   AFTER

And, of course, this was a billion years ago in the time before filter apps. Now the images we see are not only altered by programmes like Photoshop, but all those gorgeous-looking celebrity pics are created by using flattering lights and cool filters. If you hear interviews by some of the really big influencers, a lot of them will happily admit that the picture they put up (which looks like they snapped it first thing as they woke up) was actually taken 50 times before they had one they liked enough to post.

It's not only that, though. I'd often get chatting to those models. I was about the same age as they were, and there's a lot of hanging around that happens on photo shoots. You might be surprised, but one thing that loads and loads of them would tell me was how often they were the ones who had been picked on at school. Yup, they were the 'freaks', the 'oddballs', 'the geeks' never the 'pretty' one. That's also something to think about, isn't it?

LAURA'S Q & A

"It's awful when people post pictures of me on social media because my nose is so massive. It's really embarrassing - in fact I'm counting the days until I can get it fixed!"

When you look at these pictures, your nose is taking all your attention. It sounds to me like you are no longer seeing yourself as part of a group of friends, or as the person you really are, or even having a cool memory of the time when the photo was taken. Instead you are judging yourself and thinking you need to match up to a particular idea of beauty (and I'll bet your friends also worry about how they look and what they wish they could change). There's a real danger that if you're always trying to manage how you look in the photos, you might miss out on the fun of hanging with your friends.

Have another look at the people around you, not airbrushed, pouting and glamorous pictures, but the real people in your world: interesting, attractive, clever, kind, creative, fascinating, loving people – regardless of how they look. You've got some time before having your nose 'fixed' is even an option for you, and take that time to have a long, hard think. Your appearance is one small part of who you are and to place so much emphasis on how you look and believe others see you means you're giving yourself a hard time for no reason, which can really knock your confidence.

Selfies and other photos

You don't have to be a professional photographer to love taking pictures. Whether you're snapping your pets, your gang, cool and quirky things you come across, your dinner or even just yourself, taking photos has never been so popular and if you have a smart phone, the chances are that your camera is one of its most used features.

Selfies are a bit different from other pics, though, aren't they? (And by selfies, I also mean group shots). In selfies people usually show only their best sides, sometimes retouched or filtered to get rid of flaws – you might have a selfie-pose that you like to practise when taking your own picture. Certain apps are just made for selfies with cute enhancements available, and some make-up companies sell special make-up for selfies. This is a million miles away from snaps taken to celebrate or remember a particular moment or event.

Many people don't like having their photo taken at all, and sometimes this is because we can't control what the camera picks up and what we see in the photo might not match up with the image we want to have of ourselves. That can be pretty hard to come to terms with.

Listen, no one has to take photos of every moment. It's fine just to be together and rely on your memories to capture those great times. You won't disappear if you're not constantly posting photos, so if you're feeling the pressure you could just leave your phone in your pocket and enjoy the moment.

So, what am I saying? 'Pretty' might feel like it only applies to some girls but it's worth remembering that there are many, many other versions of 'pretty', and also that our idea of 'pretty' is always changing. Who knows what 'pretty' will be in 50 years' time?! There are more girls and young women out there questioning these rigid ideas of what is beautiful, what is pretty and what it means to be growing up right now. Many are deciding not to go with the flow, and to embrace themselves for who they are, rather than copying a particular image or look. Have a look on the internet – you may find it inspiring. From Instagram accounts dedicated to the celebration of girls looking gorgeous with facial hair, to fashion advertising campaigns featuring stunning models who happen to have disabilities. Looking at these images may help inspire you to be more chilled or confident about your own image and how you want to look. It could be something as small as wearing Doc Martens to school because you love them, even though 'the cool girls' are all wearing trainers (or whatever the equivalent is in your school, or your life).

No one, but no one, is more attractive than someone who is confident in themselves. You may not feel confident, and – honestly – not many people do deep down inside. However, there's something to be said for plastering a big smile on your face and looking people square in the eye when you're talking to them. Ever heard the phrase *'fake it 'til you make it'*? If someone can act confident, they will come across as confident and that in itself will help them feel confident.

It's fine and healthy to care about how you look, but make it your choice – it's not about fitting a mould. If you feel good about yourself, that will massively affect how others see you. You don't need to look like anyone else (or everyone else!) and you don't need to judge how you look based on how your friends look. Make your style work for you and then put that grin on your face and go and dazzle the world!

AM I PRETTY?

AM I NORMAL?

This could also be a time when you are wondering other things about yourself and how you fit in with the world around you. You might find that as life seems to be more about fitting into different categories, stereotypes or expectations, you feel out of place. There's a lot of pressure on girls (and boys) to act in a certain way: boys don't cry/girls shouldn't get angry, girls should look and act in a certain way if they want to be pretty or popular – but when you think about these sorts of ideas they don't add up. We are all different – and that is a great thing and something to celebrate. However, that's not much comfort if you feel 'wrong' in yourself for some reason. If you feel like the way you want to be is not 'girly', you may even wonder whether something has gone wrong somewhere along the line. Is it possible to be born into the wrong body? If you are into so-called 'boys' stuff' and you hate the idea of wearing make-up, does that mean that you're not a real girl?

'I felt as though I needed to look and behave in a "feminine" way. I had my hair short, and was frequently told I was ugly by boys. As an older teenager, I became much more aware of feminism and inequality.'

'The journey from 13 to 19 was one of the most intense I've ever been on but thanks to the lessons I learned and the friends I made I'm happy to be me, here, now and as I am.'

'I had a hard time in middle school due to hitting puberty late. It made me feel self-conscious but now I understand that being flat-chested isn't the end of the world!'

The idea of your body not representing the gender you feel you are inside is one that people feel more comfortable talking about these days, and it's certainly something that will be taken seriously. The term *gender dysphoria* refers to the anxiety felt by those who identify themselves in a way that does not match the body they were born in. Some people will have felt this all their lives, for others it's a feeling that can become much stronger during the body changes of puberty. Trouble is, it's complicated – it's really natural to be wary of the changes going on and to be worried about your body changing, eventually developing into that of a woman. Childhood is pretty uncomplicated and getting older can feel like a whole mess of responsibility, pressure and stress. Plus, as we've already discussed, there can be pressure on girls to look a certain way or fit into a certain type. Transitioning gender (or taking the steps to physically change your body) is a major life decision and like all major life decisions needs careful thought and lots of discussion. This support is available (see Further Reading on page 194) and remember, this is your time to get to know yourself, there's no rush.

LAURA'S Q & A

"I think I might have been born into the wrong body. I find girly things really boring. I used to just play with the boys but now they don't want me about and I don't know where I fit in."

There can be some pretty fixed ideas about what girls and boys should be like, and pressure from family or friends can make you feel like if you don't fit in, it is your problem. You might be strong, fast and competitive and cuddly, gentle and sensitive all at the same time. I think we can all agree that it is good to be both sensitive and courageous, and neither characteristic belongs to only boys or girls.

You're at a time in your life when lots of things are shifting. Maybe you don't feel ready for all of this change. Without doubt there will be others in your class who also feel like they don't fit in. They might not be saying it because the last thing most people want to announce is that they feel different. They are likely to be keeping these feelings to themselves and this is sad because sometimes in an effort to be like everyone else, the fantastic and unique things that make us individuals can get lost or hidden.

Even though there really is no standard girl or boy, some people feel that they have been born into the wrong body and want to be the other gender or no gender at all. This can be confusing and can leave that person feeling isolated and upset. As I say about all things, the best thing to do is talk to someone you trust if you are worried. Suffering in silence never makes anything better and will make you feel more like an outsider. Although you may feel like the only person in the world going through this, I promise that other people have felt like, and are feeling like, you. Knowing you are not alone is really important.

A FINAL POINT ON BODIES IN GENERAL

There's a massive difference between something being *private* and something being *secret*. If your friend tells you that she's started her period, that's her private business, which means it is up to her who knows about it. She's chosen to tell you because she sees you as a friend and someone she can completely trust to keep her private business to themselves.

Trust your intuition with these things, but as a good rule of thumb, if someone is asking you to keep a secret about your own body, this could be cause for concern, particularly if it is an adult who is asking you, or an older child, or basically anyone who has a bit more power than you. We all know that it's not right if someone is touching us when we don't want them to. It might not be just touching your privates, though. It could be being touched elsewhere, or being asked to show your body, or even someone commenting on your body and how it is developing. If someone is making you feel uncomfortable about your body and they are telling you that you can't tell anyone else about it *this is not a secret you should keep*. It is *your* body, not theirs, and it is up to you and you alone what you are comfortable keeping private or secret. If they've said it should be secret, then they know it is wrong and it's important that you speak to someone outside the situation.

O X O X

Part 2
THE PEOPLE
AROUND YOU:
YOUR FRIENDS AND
YOUR FAMILY

SO, WHAT'S GOING ON WITH THE BOYS?

Just like us, boys go through big changes in their bodies (and their brains) when puberty strikes.

The headlines are:

THEIR VOICES BREAK (GET DEEPER)

THEIR BALLS 'DROP' AND THEIR WILLIES GROW

THEY DEVELOP FACIAL HAIR

THEIR BODIES CHANGE SHAPE AND START TO FILL OUT A BIT

THEY GROW TALLER

It's true that boys don't have to put up with periods every month, but imagine how weird it must be to start to speak and genuinely not know what your voice is doing – squeaky high, or gruffly low. The fact is that no one, but no one, is having an easy time of it: we are all trying to get through and make sense of life (adults included!). Boys are also your brothers, your friends, your dads, your uncles. They aren't an alien species. Yes, they can seem a bit daft at times, and a bit confusing at other times, but stick with them – they're often struggling, too. Oh, yes, and it is worth bearing in mind that for boys puberty can strike a year or so later than it does for girls.

Here's Dr. Maddy to help us all understand what's going on there.

DR. MADDY

The process of puberty for boys is a bit different, although there are some things that are the same for all of us – hair growing in new places, spots breaking out, feeling a bit out of sorts.

While most of the changes in girls' bodies are controlled by oestrogen and progesterone hormones, boys are mainly ruled by **testosterone** ('tess-toss-ter-own'), which controls sperm production as well as bone mass, fat distribution, muscle strength, red blood cells and sex drive. Once this starts to activate, one of the first changes is that their testicles (their balls) will start to grow, and they will start to develop pubic hair. This can start at any age from around 10 to 13 (or older). It's around this time that they suddenly start to get taller, and by the time you get to Year 11 most of the boys will be a lot taller than the girls. Their bodies also start to change shape. In the same way that girls develop waists and hips, boys get a bit more muscular and their upper bodies typically become more like an upside-down triangle – broad at the shoulders, narrow at the waist and hips.

After about a year of this, their penis (willy) will start getting bigger and their voice will get deeper (you might have heard people say that their voices 'break'). Another year or so later, they will start getting hair on their face and under their arms. This is also when sweat glands will kick in and acne or spots may start breaking through.

On an emotional level, testosterone can also make boys quite full-on to be around – more shouty, more rough, and/or more moody. It has been linked with making them more interested in sex and it also is thought to explain why they can get really competitive – even if it's just about their favourite football teams.

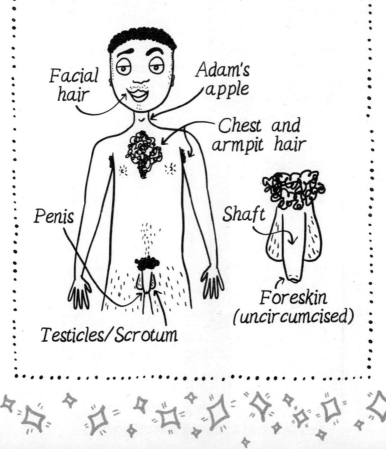

Facial hair

Adam's apple

Chest and armpit hair

Penis

Shaft

Testicles/Scrotum

Foreskin (uncircumcised)

A little note about **circumcision**: at the end of the penis is a bit of skin called the foreskin that can roll backwards and forwards over the tip. Some religions and cultures remove it from boys at birth, and sometimes a boy may need to have it removed if it starts causing difficulties. This operation is called circumcision. A boy who is circumcised is simply a boy who has had his foreskin removed.

Names for boys' bits

Add some more of your own if you like, however weird!

PENIS:	TESTICLES:
willy	balls
	scrotum

FRIENDS IRL (IN REAL LIFE)

I love my friends for their personalities, they are all different.

I love that I can be so weird, crazy, serious, sad, happy and excited around my friends.

I love my friends because they don't judge me. I can trust them and they make me laugh.

This time in your life can be so exciting, but even exciting things can be a little daunting, or overwhelming, can't they? Not only is your body changing, but the chances are at this time in your life there's a lot of other change going on, too.

If you're 10 or 11 you'll probably be thinking about secondary school, and that can seem like a massive leap into the unknown. You may be going to the same school as most of your friends, or this could be a time when your friendship group is splitting up – moving house, going to different schools – and it feels like a forced goodbye to everything you've ever known.

If you're older and are already at secondary school, you may be getting used to being 'little' again after ruling the school in Year 6. You're suddenly surrounded by loads of older kids and that can feel like a jolt after reaching the top of the pile at primary.

If you're older than that, you may well be aware that there are some big decisions you're going to have to make soon with GCSE choices looming on the horizon. These decisions can feel like they are setting up your whole life ahead of you (they needn't, but that's how it can feel). Add into the mix your parents giving you a hard time about school work, chores around the house, money, what you can and can't wear – the list goes on and on – and it can feel more and more like you're on your own.

A PROBLEM SHARED

If you're lucky, you will be able to talk about these sorts of things with someone. Talking things through helps us make sense of what we're thinking. Quite often you can feel like there's a jumble in your brain, a great big mess that you're completely unable to sort through and make any sense of.

It might be that you need to make a decision about something and you're finding it really hard, or it could be that you're struggling a bit to get your head around some of the changes going on around you. It's a funny thing, but thinking something through in your head isn't always the best thing to do. It's often when you have to put something into words that you 'hear' your own voice and find it easier to figure out what you want.

The trouble is, with all of these other changes going on, you may find that your friendships are also changing. One minute, it might seem that you're all playing in a gang together, and the next, you find yourself getting fed up with people you've hung out with for years. You're sure it's nothing to do with you – *they've* changed. It could be that they've become obsessed with boys, or keep quacking on about bands you've never heard of. Of course, it could be that they suddenly just seem really immature – they couldn't care less about having a boyfriend and all they want to do when you get together after school is make up jokes where the punchline is always poo or bum and you're just *so* over that.

It's a hard time. We've talked about how it can feel if you're not developing at the same rate as your friends or classmates and, whether you are an early bird or a later starter, it can be equally tough if you're feeling like the odd one out. To be honest, even if you're bang in the middle and your group all seems to be developing in a similar way, the fact remains that you are still experiencing these things for yourself, having your own reactions to your own individual situation – just because you're in a group, it doesn't follow that you'll all be feeling the same way about what's going on around you.

WHO'S IN YOUR CIRCLE?

Doodle in your friends or family and put yourself in the middle.

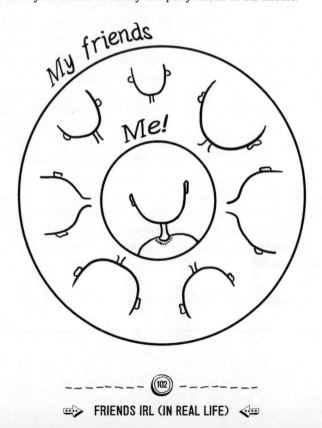

BEST FRIENDS FOREVER?

I don't really have a best friend; I have a few very good close friends in and out of school.

My best friend is a boy – he's really nice and funny.

Even your friendships can be the source of stress and bad feelings. Your friends can get on your nerves and if you don't have one, you may feel real pressure to have a BFF – Best Friend Forever. That's just it, though. There's no right or wrong here but for some reason the idea that girls have to have a best friend has become a big thing. I don't think anyone really expects boys to have exclusive best friends. It can feel like everywhere you look – not just in real life, but books, films, your favourite TV shows everyone's banging on about having a best friend. Life isn't that straightforward, though, is it? In reality, not everyone has one – and not everyone wants the best friend that they have. Some of us are more naturally drawn to hanging in a group. Having different friends who reflect your different interests is no bad thing. You shouldn't feel you're on your own if there's not a bestie in your life – there are good points and bad points about having just one person to do your thing with.

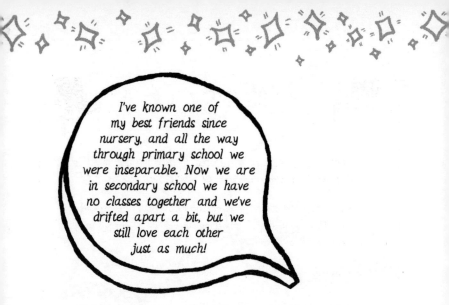

I've known one of my best friends since nursery, and all the way through primary school we were inseparable. Now we are in secondary school we have no classes together and we've drifted apart a bit, but we still love each other just as much!

Sometimes a best friend can be a tricky thing to manage – you can feel you've become tied to them – they might not like it if you want to hang out with other people, or you could feel that you are going in different directions and aren't really into the same things any more. If your friend doesn't make you feel good about yourself and doesn't encourage you in your interests (even when they're different from hers), that can be hard to handle. The truth is, the most solid friendships can change over time as we grow and develop.

This might be the time when you start to realise that actually you don't share interests any more. You might not want to play the games you used to play together, or talk about the things that you've always nattered about. There's nothing wrong with growing apart from someone. You may feel under real pressure to pretend you haven't changed, or aren't changing in a way that takes you away from her, but it's important to be true to yourself. If you want to try new things, a good friend should encourage you – so be kind and gentle, but be firm. You're not bound together for life.

LAURA'S Q & A

"I think I'm pretty popular but I haven't got a best friend. Is this because of something about me?"

Not at all. I think the idea that everyone should have a best friend is an idealisation (an idea of something perfect) rather than a true reflection of life as it really is.

Perhaps you want a best friend so much that it's getting in the way of appreciating the friendships you do have. That's really understandable – if you think about it, for most of us our first ever relationships are part of a pair: a mother and a baby. Pretty quickly, though, we start to develop relationships with other people because we are social creatures and because we need different things from different people at different times.

Try to focus on the friendships you have, and build on those where you feel you have a good connection. You might see that actually they add up to a great group of people and the idea of having a single best friend becomes less important. Even people who speak of having soulmates or best friends will still have other friends, because there are lots of different parts in all of us that make connections with different people.

GOOD FRIENDS

Friends should make us feel *good* about ourselves. A good friend should always 'have your back', which means they watch out for you and take care of you.

My friends get really annoying when they take jokes too far.

Some of the people I class as 'friends' I'd quite like to stop being around. I'm still trying to work out how to do that.

Another thing that good friends should do is big you up. I don't know why, but we can all feel kind of awkward about letting people know good things that have happened to us, or things we have achieved that make us feel really proud – from winning a prize in sports to being able to do an amazing French plait or finally mastering a cartwheel. There's nothing wrong in feeling proud of something you've done, learned or are just naturally good at.

I often hear people talking about others who are 'really into themselves' but what does that mean? If it's just someone who's happy with something about themselves, surely that's a really nice thing, isn't it? Plus, being a good friend isn't just about being happy when things go well for them, it's also about letting them be happy for you. It can be really annoying when you're trying to give someone a compliment and they keep putting themselves down – I think it's because we all worry that accepting a compliment, or telling friends about some really good news or even just mentioning something we're really proud about will come across like we're too full of ourselves. Listen, there is nothing wrong with celebrating your achievements. It's not putting someone else down to be happy in yourself.

Having friends who make you feel fantastic is a great thing, but it can be hard at this time when you're all changing. You're probably much more aware now of how everyone looks: who everyone thinks looks good, and who everyone thinks doesn't. It is really natural to start checking these things out. We all hear that you shouldn't judge a book by its cover but, most of us get our first idea about someone based on their appearance. It's worth remembering the times when you have dramatically changed your mind about someone because how they looked didn't seem to match up with the person you got to know – in a good way or a bad way. Another thing you might be doing more often now is comparing how you look with how your friends look. It can be hard if you have something about you that marks you out as different in some way to the others. You might need to wear glasses, you might not be allowed to wear make-up, you could be heavier, or not developing as quickly as the others or you could even have been born with a physical difference that makes you stand out. This is a whole other area in which your friends should make you feel good about yourself, and you should make your friends feel good, too. Sometimes, though, you can get the sense that you're being judged by your friends, that they don't make you feel good. Groups of girls can be pretty harsh, especially when someone is a bit different or sticks out in some way.

It's not just how you look that can make you feel like this. It might be more to do with the sort of stuff you're into. If you've got something in life you're really passionate about, from a subject at school, to a sport or a hobby, a good friend won't make you feel weird about it. They may not get it, they may not share your interest, but they should still understand that it's important to you.

Saying Sorry

One of life's great skills is learning how to say sorry. I can still remember a time years ago when my best friend told me I'd upset her. I'd been joking about her mum (I know! I broke the golden rule: never diss someone's mum!) and although I didn't mean it badly, I'd gone on a bit too long and crossed the line from funny to offensive. When she plucked up the courage to tell me I'd hurt her feelings I wanted to disappear – I still vividly remember the feeling of shame that washed over me and being unable to meet her eye. I knew straight away that I needed to say sorry, and I needed it to mean something to her. It was hard, but I made myself look her in the eye and tell her how sorry I was. It came from my heart and I meant it. That's what a sorry should do, otherwise it doesn't really mean anything. If you need to say sorry, do it in person if possible, or at least use your phone to make a call – not a message or a video. You've done something wrong, you need to suck it up and admit it, even if it's a hard thing to do. I asked my friend what I could do to make it better and she just wanted to know I wouldn't do it again.

It may be that making it better will require something more from you than a promise not to do the thing again. In some cases, if you're truly sorry you can't just say it, you have to take responsibility by making amends. Even if you can't take back whatever it was that you did, you can show you are sorry by doing what you can to make things right again.

Sometimes, though, I think we all find ourselves saying sorry and it doesn't actually mean that much because although we think we're doing the right thing, we're not really truly 'sorry-I'll-never-do-it-again' sorry. We are just admitting that our behaviour hasn't been great. Sometimes instead of saying sorry – or as well as saying sorry – we could say thank you.

For example, if you're late to meet your friend, and she's been waiting, instead of 'sorry I'm late, the bus didn't come' (which makes it all about you) you could try 'thank you for waiting for me, you're a great friend' (which makes it more about her in a nice way). Another example could be instead of 'sorry for going on about myself, I'm just so cross with my brother I needed to get it off my chest' you could try 'thank you for being such a great friend and a good listener. Next time I promise I won't go on so much.' It's not right for every 'sorry' but it's a great thing to bear in mind!

I don't like it when my friends keep secrets from me.

I like to mess around with my friends and be goofy! It makes me mad when they lie to me, though, and when they criticise me it makes me feel cross and frustrated.

FALSE FRIENDS AND FRENEMIES

The confusing thing is that sometimes we can really like someone even though we know deep down that they aren't a good friend. Some days they're really chatty, but other times they seem to enjoy blanking you or even actually make you feel bad. It's so hard because there's something there that you really like and when you are getting on you really feel like this person is your best friend in the whole wide world. (They're probably the ones that your mum makes a face about when you mention their name.)

It's hard when you like someone and the friendship isn't an even balance of you liking them and them liking you. But being someone's friend isn't about pleasing them all the time or always doing what they want to do. If this sounds familiar and you have someone like this in your life, maybe have a think about this friendship. Particularly if they encourage you to do things that you're not comfortable with – being mean to others, bullying, breaking school rules, doing daft stuff that you know is wrong when you're together – and saying you're 'boring' if you won't join in. It might feel like the end of the world if you don't do what they say and they tell you you're no fun, or weak or you haven't got the guts to break the rules. Chances are, though, if you have someone like this in your life they're more of an enemy than a friend – a 'frenemy', in fact. If this sounds familiar, and you think one of your friends is really a frenemy, just keep an eye out. Be more careful around them – I'm not saying they are necessarily bad to be around, but if you know you can't really trust them, listen to your instincts and don't give them too much of yourself.

Friends should be the ones you can rely on. Good friends aren't lovely one minute and mean the next. And really good friends should never put pressure on you to do stuff you know is wrong.

This might seem like the most bonkers thing I've said, but truly, it is *better to be on your own* than to be with people who don't see how great you are and make you feel bad about yourself. Or, to put it another way – if you suspect that someone is not looking out for you and maybe even doesn't like you as you really are, then leave them to it. Walk away. It is their loss. Even if that means hanging out on your own for a while, you are honestly better off without them. You have to value yourself; you are worth more than a false friend or frenemy.

YOUR OWN WORST ENEMY?

At times we all have a little voice in our head whispering things that aren't very nice. Sometimes we are our own frenemies. It's the little voice that tells you not to put your hand up in class, that you'll make a fool of yourself, that you don't look great, that you're not a nice person, that you're not good enough. The more we listen to that voice, the louder it can get. It knows all of our worst fears and if we let it get louder and louder it can stop us in our tracks.

One way of getting this voice to quieten down is to think about those things about us that we like, that we're proud of. I'm going to challenge you to fill this page with things you like about yourself. This is your private space, so go for it! You don't have to fill it in all at once – you might just have a couple of things now, but when good things happen add them to the list and when that little voice starts bugging you again, look at this list and let yourself feel proud of who you are and all of the good things about you.

. . . .

. . . .

. . . .

. . . .

. . . .

. . . .

. . . .

. . . .

. . . .

. . . .

. . . .

. . . .

It might sound a bit cheesy, but let yourself be a good friend to yourself, too, and be *proud* of the good things in your life, whatever they are. Give yourself a mental pat on the back when you ace a spelling test or help a friend out. You may not have scored the winning goal but perhaps you made a good save. Each and every one of us has good points and bad points. If you keep repeating the bad stuff in your head that can become the whole story, and it's not.

FRIENDS IRL (IN REAL LIFE)

LAURA'S Q & A

"I feel like I'm just a massive drag to be around and I haven't got any real friends. I'm not particularly good at lessons, and I don't do much at home. I don't think I really fit in anywhere."

Imagine you heard someone else being described the way you've talked about yourself here – I bet you'd think it was really unfair and quite right, too. No one deserves this, so the first and most important thing you need to do is have a think about how you feel about yourself, and to make a decision to treat yourself better.

I suggest you start small and think about the things that you enjoy, or when you feel most peaceful, or even what makes you excited, angry, lively. What do you admire in other people and how might you be able to develop those qualities in yourself? Reflect on your achievements, when you have succeeded at something in or outside of class. Can you run fast, draw well, make jokes, tell stories, be a good listener, is there a subject you enjoy, do you love listening to music, inventing, dreaming, working things out? ... I could go on and on but you get the picture.

You could write these things down in a 'me' scrapbook. This can be a collection of your thoughts, things you like and value, scribbles and doodles, photos, things torn from magazines, wish lists, records of achievements, etc. It can be whatever you want it to be and it will be yours, for you as a celebration of you.

Have a think about what you might like to achieve – joining in with an after-school activity could be a good start. Look at what's on at your school and in your area and see what you like the look of. →

Be brave, get yourself signed up and go for it. You will meet new people, learn something new and potentially develop your interest and skills. Once you have started to build this clearer picture of who you are and stopped giving so much air space to the internal bully you'll start becoming a better friend to yourself and I bet that others will want to be your friend, too.

I also wonder if there is someone you can talk to over time about these feelings? Maybe there is someone in the support team at school or in your family. It might be difficult to talk to people you are closest to – sometimes we need someone a bit further away to listen and help us get things clear in our heads. There might be a counsellor in your school or you could ask your doctor to put you in touch with local services in your area where you could meet with someone trained to listen and think with you about just how down you've got on yourself. Have a look at the websites listed on page 194 of this book, like www.youngminds.org.uk for good advice on looking after yourself and developing your self-esteem.

BULLIES

I get bullied a lot because of how I look (people ask if I'm transgender); people think I'm different to them.

Sometimes I pick on other people for being rude to my friend.

FRIENDS IRL (IN REAL LIFE)

If there's someone who is picking on you or encouraging others to give you a hard time, that's really rough. If this is happening at school, most have an anti-bullying policy and even if your school doesn't, the way it should work is that you tell your parents, they tell the school and the whole thing gets sorted. You might have a zillion reasons in your mind why you *can't* say anything: it will just make it worse; you'll get others into trouble; no one will believe you; who should you tell? But chances are you need some help here. If you can't talk to your parents, tell a teacher. If you can't tell the teacher, talk to the nurse, the TA, the Year Head. If your parents aren't around or you feel like you can't talk to them, is there someone else in your family who looks out for you?

> *The only time I picked on someone was when I was way younger and that was only because they did it to me, but now I know that is wrong.*

> *Someone has picked on me because I'm friends with someone they don't like.*

Whether you know you've messed up, or even if you know you've done nothing to cause this attention, you do not deserve to be made miserable by someone else or a group of people. If you have done something wrong (told a friend's secret/broken their phone/been messaging with their boy, whatever it is...) say sorry and make sure they know you mean it. If it's still causing problems then it sounds to me like this has now become more about them picking on you, and nothing about what, if anything, you may have done. It could be that you have no idea why this person/these people are so intent on making your life hell. That's why you need to get other people involved.

LAURA'S Q & A

> *"There's a girl in my class who really gets on my nerves. I know it's not right, but I've been giving her a hard time. I'm worried she's going to report me."*

You seem to be really struggling with this girl, and I wonder if underneath your anger you are feeling something else. Sad? Hurt? Even a bit envious?

It sounds to me like you know you're not being fair to this girl. You obviously want to do something about the situation and that's great. We all get caught up in tricky situations with other people and it can sometimes take a while to step back and realise we're not happy with what we are doing. On a practical level, could you step away when you find yourself becoming angry with this girl?

Maybe there is something about this girl that touches a nerve with you. Perhaps she seems to have something that deep down you want for yourself – not necessarily an actual thing (like the latest phone) but perhaps she's good at something you're not so confident in, or she has friends or family that seem more appealing than yours.

We can all feel envious when we wish we had what we see others getting. This feeling can grow and because it feels so uncomfortable we want to be rid of it. To do this we might try to spoil that thing, so we don't have to be faced with what we don't have.

People picked on me because I am adopted.

I have been picked on because of my weight but I have never picked on someone else.

I have been picked on by my brother many times but I know why – because I also do it to him.

Someone picked on me but I just ignored them and they stopped.

If bullying is happening somewhere else – at a club, down at the park, even in your family – the same thing applies. Figure out the best person to speak to and let them help handle the situation. The longer you listen to the bullies, the further they'll dig themselves inside your head. Please, don't let them have that power over you. I'm going to say it again – you do not deserve to be treated badly. This is so much more about those who are doing the bullying needing to have power or control over someone else because deep down inside they feel rubbish about something in their own lives. It's not your job to be understanding, though, but it is something you need to speak out about.

LAURA'S Q & A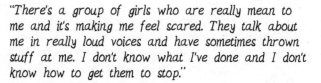

"There's a group of girls who are really mean to me and it's making me feel scared. They talk about me in really loud voices and have sometimes thrown stuff at me. I don't know what I've done and I don't know how to get them to stop."

I am really sorry to hear this is happening and can recognise just how frightening and miserable this situation is. What is really important is that you don't let this chip away at your confidence, or get in the way of you getting on with your life.

You say you don't know what you've done or how to get them to stop, but the point is that bullies will pick on people for their own reasons, and it's not about what you have or haven't done. What you can do is to get help in coping with this. Think about who there is in your life you can talk to – this could be a family member or someone at school; a teacher, mentor or school counsellor; a friend or club leader. Make a plan of what to do about these girls so that you feel stronger and their behaviour is dealt with. By taking control of the situation you will feel less helpless and hopeless.

Imagine there is a source of energy between you and them. At the moment, they have most of the energy so you feel weak and unable to stand up for yourself. They are banking on you not saying anything and by going along with this they get to keep the power. You need to take back your energy and getting a support team together will help you become brighter and more confident again.

I've got one last thing to say about friends and that is that a friendship is a two-way thing. There's been a lot in this section about how you may feel if you have a best friend, or how you may feel if you don't. How you might struggle because your friends aren't what you want them to be, how you may feel if you don't have many friends or how you might have outgrown the friends you have. I've said a few times about how your friends should be the ones who pick you up, who have your back, who make you feel fantastic about yourself. Well, that's a two-way thing. You also need to think about what sort of a friend you are. Whether you have just one or two close friends, or hang out in a big gang, you also need to be a good friend to others. Do you treat your friends well? Do you support them and encourage them in all that they want to do and be? When it comes to friends, do as you would be done by.

THE WONDERFUL WORLD OF ONLINE

Friends, are, of course, not just your classmates or the other kids who live in your area. And 'hanging out with friends' doesn't necessarily mean heading off to the local swings or cafe after school. It can mean getting together online. The joys and the pitfalls of the internet are very well known, but I still want to mention some stuff here.

I use social media, and so do most of my friends. I enjoy reading stuff online and following people I know, and some I don't, to see what they have to say, what stuff they use, what images they like creating and posting online. It is a great thing. (It's also the most efficient way of wasting a whole afternoon that has ever been thought up!) It lets everyone get involved, regardless of who you are, where you are, what you look like, what your interests are – there's somewhere for you online. It has made it possible for a singer in their bedroom to become a global megastar, an aspiring author to have her fan fiction read by thousands, or a beauty addict fangirl to become a YouTube sensation through vlogging. It feels like it makes anything possible.

> Sometimes I feel left out because I'm the only one that doesn't go on social media.

> I would like to have a YouTube channel but my mum won't let me because she says people could leave horrible comments about me.

However, what this means is that there is a lot of power there and that power can do as much harm as it can do good. You need to be careful around that much power because no one person can ever be in full control of it. What we all need to do is *take care to protect ourselves*. There are some truly tragic tales of children

I go on apps and games and research for my homework but my mum always checks what I go on.

and young people (and even older people) who walked into dangerous situations through meeting strangers online. There are equally tragic tales of those for whom online bullying took the joy out their worlds – online or otherwise.

There are loads of good places to go online that give sound advice on safety (see page 194). Here are a few good tips.

WHAT YOU'RE PUTTING OUT THERE: YOUR PROFILE, YOUR PICTURES, YOUR INNERMOST THOUGHTS AND DREAMS AND YOUR NERDIEST MOMENTS

Your profile online (on a game site, on social media, or anywhere else you may spend time) needs some thought. You might want to use it to define your online self but be really careful about giving out too much personal information (where you live, where you go to school, where you hang out). There are a few reasons why this is a bad idea. First and foremost, no matter how careful you are, you really don't know who could be reading it. You might be on a safe site where it's mates only, but you are still not completely in control of who can read what you post. Friends have friends, who have friends… The information in your profile could be used by a stranger pretending to be someone they think you'll like and trust, or it could be used to work out where you live. Always take care when giving out personal information such as your name, your address or your school. Even if you're chatting to someone you know or you think you know, you don't know who else could be checking it out – the internet is a public place!

It's also a good idea not to use a picture of yourself for your profile pic – make it your pet, your favourite band, or search up an image that you think is a great reflection of who you are.

Be aware when you're posting pictures of yourself. Say you've been playing around with make-up and you've taken a selfie where you think you look fab (and a lot older than you are). Would you want a stranger to see that version of you? Equally, that TikTok of you and your best mate re-enacting cheesy videos? That will be there forever, which is a loooong time. So think about what you're posting. Not only the funny/ weird pictures – we've all posted some of those! – but comments, too. Think back just three years – the clothes you liked wearing, the books you read, the music you loved – are you into the same stuff now? I doubt it. Whatever you're raving about online now will be searchable forever. I know it sounds like I'm saying DON'T, DON'T, DON'T and you probably think I just don't get how much fun can be had. I do, but be mindful of what you're doing. Think before hitting 'send'.

EXTRA-SPECIALLY CAREFUL

All of this applies doubly to social media. If you're on social media (and strictly speaking if you're under 13 you shouldn't even *be* on most sites) remember, it is public – there are no two ways about it. Check out your privacy settings or account settings so you know exactly who can see what you're posting online. Make sure only friends are able to see your stuff. This doesn't mean the end of your social life online – you'll still get the friend requests and messages, it just means that *you* are the one making the choices about who gets to see what you're posting.

I have had a bad experience on Instagram because people think it's OK to bully me about how I look.

PEOPLE YOU DON'T ACTUALLY KNOW IRL (IN REAL LIFE)

Making friends online can be a fantastic thing. For many, it is a way of making contact with new and interesting people. If, for whatever reason, it's hard for you to get out and about, there are friends to be made online. If the person you feel you've become at school isn't the person you feel you are inside, online you might find you can be who you want to be. You have the ultimate say in what you present to the world and you don't need to be defined by your body, how you look or how others see you. It's up to you to be whichever version of yourself you feel most comfortable being.

The trouble is, this also means that whenever you meet someone or make a friend online you *never really know who they are*. There is a lot of chat about 'stranger danger' online. There are tales (some of which are true) that go around about weirdos who 'groom' young people. Grooming means they take their time to make a relationship and build up trust. It's a scary and worrying thought, I know, but it is a serious point. You should never get into a relationship online with someone who tells you not to tell anyone else about the fact that you are communicating with each other. (Actually, this point is just as true for real life as well.) If someone is asking you to keep them as a secret this should ring a massive warning bell. If someone wants to know you they should be OK with anyone in your life knowing about them. If you make a friend online and they ask you to keep them secret, don't even ask questions: block them.

Even though most people you may end up chatting with will probably be exactly who they say they are, you still need to take care. The number one rule is you *never arrange to meet up with someone you've met online* and don't know in the real world without taking a trusted adult with you, even if that means waiting until someone is free to come along with you. This isn't about you being a child; exactly the same advice is true for adults. Make sure you are both meeting them in a public place. Not only does it mean that if there is any funny business going on there will be plenty of other people around, but also, if it is somewhere public, you're not giving away clues about where you live if they turn out to be someone you never want to see again.

You could ask your mum to take you to meet up at a cafe (for example) and she could sit at another table. Or, if you've met in a gaming room and you're both planning on going to the same fan event, get your mum or dad to take you. Or your uncle, aunt, godparent, mum's friend – whoever you are comfortable with.

NEVER, EVER, EVER agree to meet at someone's house if you don't know them in the real world (even if they are a friend of a friend).

If the person turns out to be who they said they were – hip, hip hooray, a new friendship is made. If they are a bit dodgy you've kept yourself safe. If your online friend doesn't like the idea of meeting in a public place, that should set off some alarm bells. These are all very standard ways of protecting yourself and if they have a problem with that, it may be that they are not who you think they are.

SNEAKY LOCATION SETTINGS

When you use your mobile phone or download an app it often pings up with a message asking to enable your location settings. Lots of us click yes or OK without thinking much about it. When you click yes or OK, it means your phone now knows exactly where you are. Satellites pick up your precise location – which is how you can use the maps app on your phone to get to places, for instance.

It's worth taking a moment to think about the info you're giving out when your Location/GPS settings are enabled. 'Cos it's not just your friends or family who can find out where you are – it's anyone – friend, frenemy, class pest, mortal enemies, and, of course, creeps and weirdos.

When Snap Maps launched there was a big fuss as they didn't make it clear that they'd created a new feature which meant that if you were on SnapChat anyone could see exactly where you were on a handy little map – unless you'd switched to Ghost Mode. Sneaky.

While it may seem quite cool to be able to spot your friends, it also means that if someone is hassling you or giving you a hard time (whether you know them IRL or not) they would know where you were whenever they wanted, and this could be dangerous.

It's not just SnapChat, though. If your Location/GPS settings are on when you're posting on social media, it makes your location visible. Even if it's not your exact location it's still giving out enough information for someone to be able to know roughly where you might be at that exact moment. That's worrying if the someone who's looking for you is someone you don't really know anything about.

Imagine anybody in the world being able to know where you were – does that make you feel safe? When your location settings are turned on, you may as well be carrying a big sign around with your picture, your name and all sorts of other personal information on it. Part of being safe online is protecting yourself – so make sure (do it now!) that your settings have Location off, or you are in Ghost Mode.

OTHER THINGS TO BE AWARE OF:

If someone you don't know at all and have never chatted with adds you to their contact list, *block them*. Being on their contact list can let them know when you're online. You should only accept a friend request from *someone you know in real life*. If it turns out it is someone you know who is just using another name, you'll find out sooner or later and can send them your own request.

Sometimes random emails pop into your inbox. Often these are junk emails, or 'spam'. These could be from companies that have got hold of your email address and want to advertise things to you, but they could be from people sending fake emails to trick you into replying. They can get hold of your email address by using special software or by hacking into sites that you might visit. If you don't know the sender it's best to delete these without even opening them. Emails can also contain really nasty images, or even viruses that will totally mess up your computer/ tablet or phone – they can wipe all your saved images/documents and may even make your device completely unusable. If you do open an email and it has an attachment, DON'T click on it. Opening attachments is a sure-fire way of letting viruses in.

As well as never opening attachments, the other thing to remember is: *don't reply*. If you do, they'll know that the email address they've tried (your email address) is real and they could keep on sending you loads of emails you don't want or need.

It's also possible to get texts from people you don't know. Be really wary of these, especially if they have any sort of attachment. If you don't know who it's from, don't open the attachment. Messages and texts can also contain viruses, and these can be activated when you hit reply and send.

You should hopefully know you need to be careful about who you give your mobile number to, but also never, ever post it online where it can be seen by anyone.

And remember, if you change your mind about having someone in your online life you can just delete them. However, that doesn't mean you should take less care – constantly having to block or delete messages you don't want can feel like you're under attack, and that is never good. It's much better to be really careful about who you let into your world in the first place.

Protect yourself by using a nickname rather than your real name when you're logging into chat rooms or forums. Think up a nickname that sums up who you are without giving away any personal details.

Remember, images can be copied, recorded and shared without your knowing, even if they're on something like SnapChat where they disappear after a few seconds. Taking a screen grab takes a nanosecond and then someone has your picture all for themselves to do with what they like. This is also true if you are on a video call – taking a screen shot is simple and easy and you won't know anything about it.

 # LAURA'S Q & A

"I was recently searching for something online when a really horrible picture popped up. I can't get it out of my head. I'm scared that more will pop up and that my parents might think I've been looking at something dodgy."

I can understand that what you have seen has upset you; you weren't expecting to see whatever you did. You might feel too embarrassed to talk about it, but talking about it with an adult who can listen and help you make sense of what you've seen will help get the image out of your head.

Try and 'replace' that image with something that makes you feel happy or calm. Find pictures that inspire you or make you feel good, and when you notice your mind wandering back to the horrible picture make an effort to think of your positive images. Over time you will replace that disturbing picture with something much healthier, but it might take a bit of time and some practice to replace it.

What you've experienced is not your fault and you need some support. Check what filters are in place to stop adult content $\longrightarrow$

popping up on your wifi settings at home. They may need to be increased or updated to reduce the risk of you seeing things that disturb you. Some pictures that are posted online actually show things that break the law, so again, it is important that you tell an adult (and if you really can't tell your parents there is probably someone at your school who is in charge of IT). They will be able to report anything that is illegal to the proper authorities, and you won't need to worry about this.

ONLINE CHATTING, MESSAGES, TEXTS AND EMAILS

The weird thing about emails, messages, texts and online chatting is that when you're writing something, you are probably thinking the words in your head as you type. You know if you're joking about something or being sarcastic, but the person reading it may not. It can be really easy to offend someone because the reader is not 'hearing' the tone in your voice. You need to think twice before hitting 'send' to make sure you've been clear about what you're saying.

People can send nasty texts and messages on purpose and that is horrible if you are on the receiving end. If you get a message that upsets you, remember, you don't *need* to reply. If you want to though, there's no pressure to respond straight away. Take a little time to decide what you want to say. It is often better to have difficult conversations face to face, even if that's hard to think about. When you're typing instead of speaking, it's really easy to get carried away saying stuff you may not even mean.

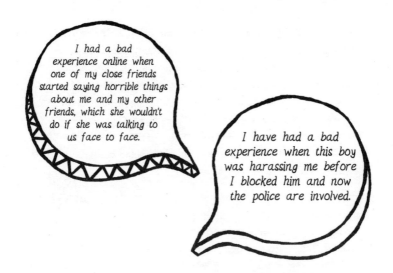

I had a bad experience online when one of my close friends started saying horrible things about me and my other friends, which she wouldn't do if she was talking to us face to face.

I have had a bad experience when this boy was harassing me before I blocked him and now the police are involved.

If you're really mad at someone of course it's *tempting* to say so online, but it will be there for all to read – is that what you want? A good rule of thumb is: never say something online that you wouldn't say to someone's face. And if you are tempted, maybe you need to have a little think about why you feel you could say it online but not in person.

If someone is giving you a hard time online, this is called cyberbullying. Just because it's got 'cyber' in front of it doesn't make it any easier to deal with. One aspect of being bullied online is that those words or pictures are there *forever*, meaning the temptation to re-read them can be pretty intense. Online or AFK (away from the keyboard) bullying is bullying. If you're getting bullied it really isn't about you. It's not because of who you are. It's about how the bully is feeling, which may be something bad that they can't handle and they're looking to take it out on someone else.

If it's happening online the number one rule is: *don't respond.* If you're getting upsetting messages, texts or emails, save them. Try not to read them over again, just stick them in a folder to keep a record in case you need it. Tell a trusted adult. You may not want to show them the messages you've received if they are really upsetting or embarrassing, but there are cases where you will need the support. If someone is sending you messages or pictures that you find disturbing – if they are violent, or scary, or sexual – this may be against the law and needs to be reported to the correct authorities.

Another difference with online bullying (as opposed to bullying in real life) is that it could be someone you don't know but have allowed into your online world. You may feel worried that you'll get in trouble for letting them contact you in the first place. I promise you, though, that the problem here is still them, not you. Everyone can make mistakes, and maybe you made a mistake letting this person into your life but don't let that fear stop you doing the right thing. Block them and tell someone what is going on.

WHEN FUN STUFF STOPS BEING FUN

Sharing on social media is a fab way of letting people know what your likes and dislikes are, what you think is cool, or bang out of order. Sometimes, though, there's a pressure to share posts – some posts specifically say that if you share them something really great will happen, and some say that bad things will happen if you don't pass them on. These are called chain posts. Before chain posts, there were chain emails, and before chain emails, there were chain letters. You see, the idea has been around for some time. Some of them are pretty harmless – 'if you share this you will have good fortune' – but some are really nasty: 'share this post if you love your mum because if you don't she will die'. I know how horrid it can be to get one of these, and how much pressure you can feel to share, or send on. There is no truth in them, though. No bad thing will happen if you don't send them on and no good thing will happen if you do. They are made up by someone far back down the chain who wants to see how far it can go. Ignore, delete or, if you're really freaked out about this and feel like you HAVE to pass it on, pass it on to an adult and explain to them why you have done this. When you're online, it can consume you. I know.

I'm as guilty as anyone of fiddling with my phone, getting hooked on games, obsessively checking social media. I know, too, that it can take me away from what is happening in my real life, around me. One of the things that can get under your skin the most and take over all your thoughts is gaming, although the fear of missing something on social media comes a close second. Both can be really addictive and that is now a recognised problem. Like all addictions – alcohol, drugs, even exercise – it is bad if it gets to the stage where you can't control it. If you're rowing with your parents about how much time you spend online, if you are getting into trouble at school for constantly checking your phone, if you feel nervous and fidgety if you can't get to a screen it might mean that this has become a problem for you and if this is the case you need to tell someone who can help.

Take time out. Turn off the screen. Look around your world – if it doesn't match the joys of online life, have a think about what you could do to make reality better for you. You are living your own life, and you have more control over it than you can possibly know.

 # LAURA'S Q & A

"Me and my friends use social media after school and for most of the evening. I get really worried that I'll miss out on what's happening when we go on our family holiday if there's no reception at the resort."

Phew! I'm exhausted just thinking about spending all day with my friends and then getting home and carrying on with the chatting. I know it's really important to have contact with your mates but it is also really important (for all of us) to have some separate time just by yourself and, of course, to have family time, too. I know it's going to feel hard not to be in touch while you're away but this might be an opportunity to have some time where you can get back in touch with other things that you like to do and the other important relationships in your life. By taking some time to be alone you get to recharge your batteries.

When you spend so much of your time on social media you might forget the other things you like doing and start to feel anxious if you're not continually using your devices. I think it might be a good idea to set a few boundaries for yourself in your day-to-day life. I suggest you experiment with delaying when you get on to your phone after school – have an hour or so to do something else, whatever floats your boat that doesn't involve a screen. I'm not suggesting that you never use your phone or device, but just balance it out a bit to give yourself some time to recover from all that social contact. We all need time to tune into our own thoughts and feelings.

The great thing about family holidays is that everyone is away from their work and other commitments so you get a chance to be together. Real-life experiences are very important for our mental and emotional well-being. Balance is everything.

DIFFICULT FEELINGS: ANGRY, JEALOUS, MEAN, MOODY, ANXIOUS & TOTALLY DEPRESSED

Some emotions are hard to deal with, whether we are feeling them ourselves, or seeing other people feel that way. It can be hard, but feeling sad, angry, jealous, worried or down is just as important to our development as feeling happy, proud, grateful, hopeful and loving. These feelings are often called negative or bad, but I don't want to use those words, because stuff we think of as bad is usually stuff we don't want. We might try and ignore bad things, or pretend they don't exist but we need to understand that our feelings are a natural response to what is going on in our lives. We need to try and figure out why we feel different emotions so we can know ourselves better, and – ultimately – be happier and more certain of who we are.

I know it may sound like it doesn't have much to do with puberty but this can be a time when all of these emotions are whooshing through you one after the other and that can be really overwhelming. Feeling emotions is part of what makes us human and our emotions are important and not something to be dismissed (like saying 'cheer up, it might never happen'). If you're feeling sad or angry or jealous or frustrated, being told not to feel that way never really works, does it? That said, if someone else is feeling bad it can be really hard to know what to say to them. It can feel easier to try and jolly them out of their 'bad' mood than to see someone who you care about feeling down.

When something gets under your skin and makes you feel really mad it can be the first step to doing something really positive. Take frustration, which is when you're annoyed because things don't go your way, or you feel blocked in some way – whether it's your dad who won't understand that your homework really can wait until you've gone up the next level on the game you're in the middle of, or your friend who keeps making silly faces when you're trying to tell her something, or the fact that you just can't shoot the ball through the net even though you've tried a billion times. Getting frustrated is natural when you feel like something is coming between you and the thing you want. Often, though, the way around this is fairly straightforward – figure out what the block is and see what you can do to remove it. However, if your anger is kicking in because of something that you feel is undeniably unfair, use all that emotion and energy to change things around you. Emmeline Pankhurst channelled her rage to campaign for women's votes at the start of the 20th century, and Malala Yousafzai was so angry that girls like her were being denied their right to education that she spoke out, and risked her life for her beliefs.

MALALA YOUSAFZAI

Rosa Parks used her anger to help kick-start the Civil Rights Movement in America – just three examples of great women using their anger to change society. That might seem a little far removed from your everyday life, but say, for example, you're angry that girls can't play in your school's football team, try using that anger in a positive way: get a petition started, go to the school council, get involved and try and make a change for the better.

We all know deep down that we should be 'happy for them' when good things happen to people we know, especially when we're close to them. Truth is, it's often a bit more complicated than that. There can be an overwhelming sense of 'why them and not me?' Own that feeling and take a good long look at who's got what you want. If your desk partner always gets the praise for work you do together, could it be that they are better at speaking up? And if so, good for them – there's no harm in letting people know when you're pleased with your work. Perhaps your brother or sister is always coming first while you are left behind them, never quite making the top spot. Do they put more hours in? Is there more you could be doing to get what you want? It might be that one of your friends always has the latest cool stuff and you wish you got as much from your parents. Well, it could be that her parents have more money to spend, or it could be that they are giving her lots of stuff but she's looking at you wishing her mum was cuddly like yours, or that her dad wasn't at work quite so much.

ROSA PARKS

What I'm trying to say is that when you are feeling jealous, make sure you're seeing the whole picture. It may be that you feel really self-conscious about speaking out, or you don't want to get up at stupid o'clock to do extra training, or even that you don't know what's happening with your friend's home life but actually she's pretty cool about sharing her good fortune with you. These are all examples, of course, but realising these things about yourself and what part you play might help you feel better.

LAURA'S Q & A

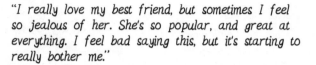

"I really love my best friend, but sometimes I feel so jealous of her. She's so popular, and great at everything. I feel bad saying this, but it's starting to really bother me."

This is tough and you're right to want to sort it out. It sounds like there's a part of you that wants what your friend has, and resents that she has it, but there's another part that loves her and wants the best for her. It is really difficult to feel two different things at the same time. Jealousy is a normal and natural part of life, admittedly one that can feel horrible and needs keeping an eye on.

Deep down we all have a basic instinct to do well. It helps us grow, become skilled and invent new ways of doing things. However, we need to make sure that the desire to succeed doesn't get the better of us and make us forget other things that are more important, like our friendships.

We all have times in our lives when we are centre stage and other times when we are the support act. Let yourself get excited about what you do and what you are good at, and be proud of your friend. Chances are that at some point she will be looking at what you have and wishing it was hers.

Finally, I want to say that although you might feel you need to hide that jealousy away, you don't. It is perfectly natural and you could say to your friend that though you love her, you sometimes feel jealous. Getting it off your chest and out of your head is an important part of starting to understand these complicated feelings.

DIFFICULT FEELINGS

We all try and mask our emotions sometimes – hiding behind a smile or making a joke. This is fine every now and then, but if 'bad' feelings build up inside they can start to hurt us.

When we are in the grip of our emotions – about-to-burst-angry or can't-stop-crying-sad – we are not feeling like our normal selves. We aren't capable of making those same sensible choices that we might make at another time and in another mood. It can be a good idea to take some time out, if possible, and do something that you know will help you relax and allow these emotions to die back a bit until you feel more in control of them. You'll know what works for you, but here are some ideas to start you off:

My soothing tips:

- *Cuddle up in bed*
- *Go for a walk*
- *Do some gaming – probably not something competitive or where you have to get on to the next level*
- *Read a book*
- *Get creative – build something or try a bit of craft or make a picture. If you're not feeling inspired, get your art supplies out and try one of those colouring books*
- *Get into the kitchen and bake or cook*

Add some more of your own:

....

....

....

....

....

....

....

....

....

....

LAURA'S Q & A

"I get very cross sometimes with my friends or my family but I'm worried that if they knew how I feel they will be upset with me and I don't want that."

Anger is usually a reaction against something but it can rise up in unexpected ways so we don't even know why we are so angry. Remember, though, like all feelings there is always a reason and we have to become our own best detectives in working out why here and why now. I wonder what might be happening when you get cross. You might be feeling wronged or misunderstood and anger arises as a defence against this. There might be something that annoyed you a while ago and was never put right, so when you sense a similar situation arising again you are quicker to get angry. I think it could be really helpful to think about what it is that is winding you up so much and perhaps this is something you could then talk about with others.

We all get angry and, as Sophie says, it can be used to make positive change and fight injustice. Imagine anger like a guard dog whose job it is to protect us when we are threatened. Like a dog, anger needs to be looked after and treated with respect. The trouble is, if we are told that anger is not nice and should not be allowed out then, in the same way as a dog that gets locked up and neglected, anger can become more difficult to manage. We need to rely on our anger for those times when we really need it, but we don't want it to take over where it is not welcome. If we try and squash angry feelings we can find ourselves getting angry without understanding why.

UNDERSTANDING OTHERS

If you're feeling jealous, angry, sad or frustrated it's good to spend
time thinking about why this may be and what (if anything) you can do
about it, but often I think we can be tempted to lock it away somewhere
because of the worry that feeling something 'bad' makes us 'mean'.

And what's it all about? I've heard a lot about mean. How such-a-body
has been 'so mean' or how it's mean to say this or do that. Being mean
is horrid – when someone is mean to you it can make you feel silly,
or sad or just really upset. And, when you're mean to someone else
it might feel great at first but perhaps later you might feel silly, sad or
just really upset as well. If you know you're being mean, try and catch
yourself, and think about why you wanted to hurt or upset that person.
Was it because something had happened to upset you and a part of you
wanted to pass that upset on to someone else?

Once you've tried this with yourself, try it with others you feel are
being unfair or unkind to you – the nasty girl in your class, the snappy
teacher, your mum when she's telling you for the billionth time to tidy
your room. If you can figure out why you feel they're being mean it
will probably make their behaviour seem a lot less hurtful or annoying.
Have you heard the words 'empathy' and 'sympathy'? They sound
similar but the meaning is actually quite different: sympathy is feeling
sorry for someone; empathy is when you put yourself in their shoes and
try to feel what they are feeling. It might not make what they're doing
OK, but it will help you to understand them and not take it so much
to heart.

KEEPING IT ALL IN

You know that feeling you get, when something is bothering you and
you just can't tell anyone? You're probably thinking it's the biggest,
baddest secret in the whole wide world. You might be worried because
your mum and dad are always fighting, or because you can't get your
head around what you're supposed to be doing in Maths. Maybe

someone who you thought was your friend has started blanking you, or even picking on you. It might even be you who's picking on someone, and you don't really know why: you feel like a horrid person, but you can't stop yourself.

Either way, it's a bit like someone is blowing up a balloon, right in your tummy. It gets bigger, and bigger, and bigger.

All you can do is worry that it will pop inside you. You know that whatever is inside it is messy and mean and that it won't feel nice when it pops. You dread it. It feels like if you tell anyone that you have this balloon, then that, too, could make it pop. It won't.

Here's what will happen if you tell someone about the balloon, and what is filling it up with the bad stuff and making it grow inside you: you'll let a bit of that air out, that mucky dirty air that is filling you up inside and making you feel rubbish. A little bit of that will come out, and it will make you feel better, I promise.

So find someone, find a good grown-up. I have written the words 'trusted adult' throughout this book, but only you know who that would be in your life – it might be your mum or dad, it may be a cool auntie, or that nice teacher, or even your mate's mum. Whoever it is, tell them, and let them help. I bet they've been through it, or they know someone who has, and they'll be able to gently let out that bad air until the balloon inside you deflates and you feel like you again.

LAURA'S Q & A

"I feel down all the time, like I just can't be bothered with anyone or get excited about the sort of stuff I used to like. I'm fed up with feeling miserable but I can't shake myself out of it and maybe I need some help?"

I'm sure you know that we all get down sometimes and don't feel like being with other people. This is normal and can be a sign that you need some time to yourself to snuggle up on the sofa in front of a movie, or take your mind off everyday life altogether by going out for a cycle ride or a long walk. However, sometimes this mood can get stuck and take over, and we can find ourselves feeling really unhappy, angry, tired or hopeless most of the time.

Down moods can sometimes become what is called depression, which gets in the way of getting on with life and your normal relationships – friends, boyfriends, girlfriends and family. If you are feeling like this you need to try and be honest and open with yourself as much as anyone else. A good way of sorting things out in your own head is to write about it. It could be in the form of a letter (you don't need to send it, but writing it down may help) or a poem – even a song. Lots of the best songs out there have been about trying to work through problems. Another great thing to do is to keep a diary of your innermost thoughts and feelings.

Any of these may help give your feelings a form which may make it easier to make sense of them. You could even try making up a story about someone in your situation, and let your imagination wander to try and find different solutions. If you're not much of a writer, try drawing or painting, or even dancing – whatever makes you happy.

You also need to be talking about this with someone else – with your parents, or a good friend, a trusted adult someone outside of your head who may help give you another viewpoint. It might be a long and ongoing conversation and not something that can be fixed overnight, so give yourself a chance and don't be hard on yourself if it's taking a bit of time to feel like 'you' again.

DR. MADDY

From a medical perspective, puberty is all about how the body reacts when it starts to produce certain hormones. We talk quite a lot about specific hormonal changes in other chapters – how they have an impact on your body in different ways. The fact is that while these body changes are going on, our thoughts and feelings are also affected. I bet you've heard people talking about moody teenagers – right? Well, it isn't surprising because the hormones that are doing things like starting your periods, giving you spots and changing your breasts are also playing with your mind. This can make you feel angry, confused, tired, frustrated and really down – sometimes all in the space of five minutes. However, ongoing depressed feelings can become too big a deal to cope with on your own. There are a number of different ways of treating depression. If you've spoken about this with someone, as Laura suggests, and you feel you need something more, ask for an appointment with your doctor.

This could also be a time when you may find yourself using words like 'stressed' and 'anxious' a lot more than you ever did before. Stress and anxiety (being anxious) are often used to mean the same thing, but in fact they are different. Both are emotions that you could feel when faced with a potentially worrying or threatening situation, but stress is a response to actual pressure (you're sitting a test and your mind goes blank) and anxiety is the worrying-about-it bit, which can start before or continue after the situation is resolved (you can't sleep for days before the test and spend days afterwards worrying that your answers

DIFFICULT FEELINGS

were all wrong). When you feel stressed, it's often helpful if you can take some time away from the situation (see the soothing tips on page 143). If, however, stress has ballooned into anxiety, this may feel a little more overwhelming.

Should I...?

What if...?

When will...?

What can I do...?

Can't forget...

I need to...

I can't...

Must remember...

What will they say...?

When people talk about feeling anxious they are often describing how they feel about something they are facing that is bad and unwanted, and this state (anxiety) can become a problem if it gets out of control. Remember, feelings of anxiety are a natural response to a situation where there is some pressure – when we want to do something well and when something matters to us. If you're not confident about a test it's perfectly natural to be worried; if you're going to be away from home, and it's something you've not done before, of course you'll worry about missing your family and how you'll get to sleep without your 'stuff' around you; or, if you've had a falling-out with friends you may well be concerned they'll be talking about it with each other. These are reasonable responses – although it should be said that life is full of opportunities and just because it's normal to feel a little worried or scared before doing something for the first time, that's not a reason never to try anything new.

WORKING THINGS THROUGH

Learning how to deal with our feelings is a life's mission. As I've said, some feelings are difficult and you might worry that if you are struggling it's because of something about you – that you're not coping as well as others seem to. You might have tried your 'soothing tips' and they haven't worked for you. What then? Does this mean there's something wrong with you? Well, no. As we know, some things in life can't be made better by waving a magic wand, sadly. Sometimes things feel hard because they are hard: this is part of life. However, they don't have to take over your life or define who you are. While in the middle of a stressful situation you might have to accept that you are going to feel bad, but that feeling won't last forever. Working through a stressful situation can ultimately be a really important way to learn about yourself and develop your emotional strength.

Saying that, if you find you are anxious a lot of the time, or you get anxious about things that don't seem like a big deal, then anxiety might become a problem and can make life feel pretty miserable. You might notice you always have a jittery feeling in your stomach, or feel it is impossible to join in with friends or activities that others seem to breeze through. If you find yourself in this position it may be that you need some help to work out what's going on.

LAURA'S Q & A

"I feel anxious all the time. I get really stressed out by loads of things and my mind feels like it can't stop worrying about stuff, even if it's not a big deal. What can I do?"

First things first: it sounds like you are getting stuck in a cycle of worrying and the important thing is to try and break the cycle so that you can get some relief. Then have a look at whether there is something to be done about the things that are bothering you.

There are techniques that you might use to get some control over the worries. For example, write down what is on your mind and decide what needs immediate attention. It might be that some of what you worry about is beyond your control and so those things can go to the bottom of your list. Put the things that you can do something about first, then choose one of these to give your attention to. We all have busy brains and it is likely that the other items on the list will try to demand your attention, but you need to put them in their place, which is further down the list.

You might make a realistic and a fantasy list of solutions — put down whatever you want, but put into action something you can actually do to make things better. If you can cross something off your list it will give you a sense of satisfaction, and you'll have got one over on the worry cycle. Action is the enemy of worrying. It will take practice and support to help you master this, but stick with it because you can gain some skills and won't have to spend all your energy worrying.

$\longrightarrow$

However, this technique won't work if you have become so completely overwhelmed by worries, and you've got such big and frightening feelings in your body, that in that moment you can't think at all. If you're at this stage, you may feel like it is making you ill, or you are struggling to breathe properly when the worries take over your mind (this is called having a panic attack – see the box below on coping with one). This state doesn't last and it can help to think of it as a wave of panic. At the worst point you are on the top of the wave and though it can feel like it won't end, remember that all waves eventually lose their energy and wash up on the shore. It will come down and you will get through this.

Tips for coping with a panic attack

✦ First, recognise what is happening to you and know that it will pass, repeating this to yourself can be calming.

✦ Slow down your breathing by concentrating on the OUT breath and focusing like you are blowing into a balloon. Breathe IN through your nose and OUT through your mouth, making your out breath last longer as you slowly calm down.

✦ It will take a bit of time to bring your breathing back to a manageable level, but it will come down.

✦ When you are back to a more manageable state, talk to someone you trust about what happened, what you think might have led to the panic attack and the things that are on your mind.

It can help to put a limit on the time you give to worrying every day, so that it doesn't start to take over. If you feel you've got a lot to worry about, give yourself 20 minutes a day to talk things through, taking your worries one by one rather than letting them merge into one huge problem. At the end of that time, do something different to grow your healthy mind muscles through practising positive experiences: take up a new sport or club activity, ride your bike fast through some muddy puddles, run up and roll down a hill, shake it all out on the trampoline, play a musical instrument or compose a tune, create your own dance routine, do a drawing of the view in front of you. Those are just some suggestions but there are loads of things you could do to get you into your body and out of that worrying mindset.

LIFE AT HOME

Family life can be complicated for many reasons. Parents can find it hard to face the fact that their little baby is growing up and becoming a person in their own right, and if you're being treated as if you don't have a mind of your own (or the brains you were born with) it can feel frustrating and unfair. Up to now you may not have really thought about your parents as people in their own right – just as Mum or Dad.

Everyone in a family (regardless of how that family is made up) can end up playing a role. The parents become 'Mum' or 'Dad'. Their main job is to be there, but also in that role they make the rules and make sure those rules are stuck to. There are, of course, other parts to that role – giver of cuddles, cheerleader, cook, cleaner, and – fingers crossed – confidant (which means someone you know you can always talk to and trust, no matter what).

However, the chances are that you have been given a role, too: 'Good Girl', 'Happy Girl, 'Clever Girl', 'Pretty Girl' or even, sadly, 'Naughty

Girl'. If you have siblings, you may have each been given different roles, but even if there's just one of you, you'll also have your role.

You may be comfortable with that but you might find that now you are getting to know yourself you are starting to struggle with the role you've been given. Perhaps you found it a bit tricky to start off with at school but are now getting great marks, or you could feel like being 'good' has become a bit strangulating and desperately want to kick off a bit, just to make it clear you are your own person. It might be that you have an older sister who's always been the pretty one or the funny one, but now there's no room for you to be pretty or when you crack a joke everyone just looks a bit surprised.

How can you let your family know who you are, if all they see when they look at you is your role? It's hard to do without getting into arguments and shouting becoming involved. Perhaps this is why this can be such a fraught, or tense, time. You want to explore the world around you and develop your independence. You may not want to be treated the same way you have always been. You're also developing another network around you – your friends and you might want to spend more time with them right now. You may feel like they are the only people in your life who 'get' you.

TYPICAL FAMILY?

It could be that when you're at home it feels like you're constantly arguing with your family – your mum is always shouting, your dad doesn't understand that you're growing up, your siblings are driving you nuts. That's if you live with your mum, dad and have brothers or sisters in the first place – you may have a different family set-up: living with step-parents and you miss your 'real' mum or dad or your family may involve step-siblings who get on your nerves and you never chose to live with them in the first place. Perhaps there's a new baby in the house taking all the attention or if you live with a carer/guardian this could be a tricky time to open up and allow them the privilege of really knowing the you inside. There's an old saying I'm sure you've heard: 'you can choose your friends but you can't choose your family!' Add into the mix the fact that not all families follow the same pattern and your set-up might feel really different to that of your friends.

The point I'm trying to make is that there is no such thing as a typical family. Our family is essentially who we live with and each of us makes our own version of 'typical' based on that.

Typical families?

You may live with both of your birth parents, but one of them could be away a lot with work and you feel like the odd one out because your friends' parents are always around. You might live with grandparents, aunts or uncles who all get involved in your business. You may have loads of siblings and feel like you're fighting for space, or be an only child and wish you had someone to squabble with. It could be that you have half-brothers or sisters who you live with, or who come and stay sometimes and you have to fit around them.

You could be adopted and never see your birth family, or have an ongoing relationship with your birth mother, father or siblings and struggle with having a different life to them. You could be living in care, with other family members, foster parents or in a residential school.

Your mum could be in a relationship with another woman or your father with another man. You may live in more than one place and feel self-conscious about it when making weekend plans with your friends.

It's not as common, certainly, but you could have a parent who has gone through a gender transition – say your dad has realised he is more comfortable identifying as a woman. It's happening more and more often, and while it is wonderful that people don't feel the same pressure to live a lie, it can be tough going through this, for adults and the kids.

That's a lot of 'you coulds' for one chapter, isn't it? And, what they all have in common is that you can be living in any one of them and know that you are safe, you are understood, you are supported and you are loved. Equally, you can be living in any one of those situations and feel misunderstood, neglected or anxious. Families, however they are made up, can be hard work. As human beings, we expect our families to be our number one support network. If that doesn't feel true for you – if your family aren't giving you whatever it is you need, or that love and support doesn't seem very obvious, it can feel harsh. As I said before, you might feel your family just don't get you like your friends do. OK, maybe they don't. That doesn't mean they don't love you, but it may feel like they don't know you, and that can leave you feeling lonely perhaps, or just plain misunderstood.

Pop your family into the blank frame.

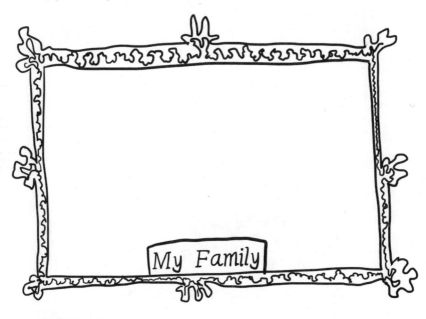

My Family

FIREWORKS

I think when you're arguing with your parents it can leave you feeling really sad deep down – even if you're convinced that you're right and they're wrong. It's really natural that there'll be a part of you that will be upset if you feel like your relationship has become a battleground. You might even find that rows are blowing up out of nowhere and when you stop to think about how it started you can't even remember. Up to this point, they've probably been the people you've been closest to all your life. We've all heard of 'Daddy's girls' and mother-daughter relationships are time-honoured for being precious. Then you chuck puberty in the mix and the fireworks can really start exploding.

LAURA'S Q & A

"Me and my mum always end up arguing. We used to get on really well and I don't know what's changed. We can't seem to have a conversation without it blowing up. Please help."

Things probably felt easier between you and your mum when you were younger as in many ways your life was simpler: what you did and when you did it was in the control of your parents. Now you're growing and starting to find out what you like, how you want to spend your time, and who you want to be with.

When you were little you probably looked up to your mum and saw her as the centre of your world. For the first few years you were completely dependent on her. As you've started to grow, and particularly during puberty, you have started to see the flaws and limitations in your mum. She has stopped seeming 'perfect' to you and has become more human. This can be painful and it might take a number of years to be able to see your mum as a human with strengths and weaknesses that you can respect regardless.

While you're going through changes, your mum is also having to adjust to you as a young woman who is developing her own ideas and identity, and doesn't need her mum in the same way. You might find yourself irritated when she talks to you like you're a little girl and she might feel irritated when you answer back. It can be hard to accept, but you still need your mum. Remember — she has been your age, too.

The main thing you both need is to keep talking and being with each other in ways that bring out the best in you both. It can feel easier to steer clear and avoid conflict, but the less time you spend together, the harder it will be to stay close. This is a situation that is clearly bothering you and though she might not have expressed it in the same way, there's a strong chance your mum is bothered, too. There's going to have to be compromise for you both.

Try talking to your mum when you're not in an argument. Have a think about how the two of you can get some time together. Is there a day when you are both around at home? You could have a film night, or take the dog for a walk. Sometimes parents and children can drift apart even when living in the same house. Just doing simple things together can really help you grow memories of good times, which can offset the struggles. There are likely to be some stormy times ahead where you really annoy each other. You can and will get through it as long as you keep talking and remember that despite the rows you love each other.

Something that may be quite hard to achieve during these years, but will stand you in really good stead as you move forward, is remembering that not only do you deep down love your parents or carers, but also that you should respect them, and they in turn should respect you. Respect needs to be earned and that works both ways. Respect them for being the people who made you and got you through to this stage. Respect what they bring to the home and their attempts to make your family work together, and you do your bit by being someone they can respect, too.

Show them that although you might want to do things differently now, you have reached your decisions by thinking them through. If you want more independence, show them they can trust you – talk to them, let them know you're not going to go daft if they let you off the leash a bit. If you get it wrong, do what you can to make it right and show them that you can learn from mistakes – they'll be much more likely to take you seriously if they see you doing your bit. (See the section on Saying Sorry on page 109.) They may well still see you as their little girl, but they need to get to know the changing you, and they can only do this if you let them in.

And finally, and I hope you're getting this message loud and clear – you shouldn't let anyone, even someone in your own family, tell you that you should do a thing, or you can't do a thing 'because you are a girl'. That respect you need to earn should be about who you are as a person, not as a girl. Your family should be championing you all the way with your hopes and dreams, your interests and your passions. Your gender, or the fact you are a girl, shouldn't come into it.

It can, though, and it does. Dads and mums have dreams about their little girls and what they want for them and sometimes these dreams can be formed from old-fashioned ideas about what is appropriate and what isn't. Your dad may joke about no boy ever being good enough for his daughter, or your mum may expect you to help more around the house than your brother. Of course you should help around the house, not because you're a girl, but because you are a member of the family and should do your share as should each family member – boys, girls, mums and dads!

As a parent myself, I've got to say we all know deep down that we can and do mess up. It can be hard to remember, but parents are also people who have lived a life separate from being a parent. However, this isn't a book about parents and their woes and struggles, it's about you.

BOYS, GIRLS OR NO THANKS?

So, the million dollar question – do you like someone? I mean … like? And if so, how would you describe it? True love? Fancying? A crush? You might read this and think NO WAY – not for me. And that is fine – skip over this section, but remember it's here if you change your mind.

> I have had a boyfriend, actually a few. I am kind of interested in boys, however my mum says I am too young to be thinking about them (but I still do).

> I do currently have a boy crush but I also fancy girls and I think I'm bisexual, or at least going through a bisexual phase.

This is the time in your life when you may start to feel really drawn to someone in a way that is something other than friendship. There's no rule about who could have caught your eye – a boy, a girl, someone older, someone famous – maybe even someone who exists mainly in your imagination. You could have crushes on more than one person at any given time or it could be that you are going out with someone, so it's moved beyond a crush.

First things first, then, and the first step is usually having a crush on someone. A crush is when you are massively drawn to someone and have a raging desire to be near them (even if you find yourself running away when they are close by). Just thinking about them could make you feel nervous, shy, embarrassed, flustered but in a way that's somehow exciting. There are lots of different types of crushes – you can have a crush on a friend who you just love being around and think of when you're not with them – daydreaming about fun stuff you could do together or having imaginary conversations with them in your head when something happens that you want to chat over with them. You might have a crush on someone you admire because you think that what they do or how they look or act is really cool. This could be someone famous but

I have a lot of fictional crushes (*ahem* James Potter *ahem*).

it could be someone at your school who you think really highly of, and you just love the way they always seem to get things right. With this sort of crush if you are in a position where you get to know them a little better, you might find that the crush-like feeling (that raging desire to be with them) dies down a little and maybe something else develops – a friendship, perhaps.

And then, of course, there is the crush you may have on someone when your daydreaming takes on a physical aspect – you want to be close to them – you imagine brushing past them in the corridor, or dancing with them at a party; you might even think about kissing them or being close in other ways. Again, this sort of crush could be someone you know, or someone don't know very well at all. You could be crushing on a singer, or an actor – some celebrity that you really like the look of. It could be a teacher or even a friend of your parents.

If it's on someone you don't know in real life (like a celebrity) you won't have the opportunity to make a real relationship with this person. In lots of ways crushing on, or fancying, a famous person can be fab. Stick their picture on your wall or in your locker. Write their name in your books and see what it looks like next to yours. Search them up on the internet. Spend hours studying that cute thing they do with their hair and melt over the soulful look in their eyes. Knock yourself out. Having this sort of crush is great. It's not going to go anywhere, it's not going to develop into something serious – you're not going to have to make any decisions so daydream away and fully enjoy it for what it is.

If, however, your crush is on someone you know, who is close to your age and who you see often, there may be a chance it could develop further. You could be crushing on a boy or a girl. Many years ago the idea that boys could be attracted to boys and girls could be attracted to girls was seen as being wrong. There were actually laws against boys being with boys. They didn't bother to make laws against girls being with girls because the very idea of girls liking each other was so unimaginable they didn't think it was worth the effort of setting laws up. Now, even if you've never had a crush on a girl, I bet you can still imagine it would be possible.

'I remember having a crush on a girl in my class when I was about 14 but I pretended to fancy people long before I actually did.'

'I'm romantically attracted to girls but not in a sexual way.'

You may feel drawn to girls but also like boys, too. Or, you could just like boys. When you are attracted to someone who is the opposite sex to you this is officially referred to as **heterosexual** and often described as being 'straight'. If you're attracted to someone who is the same sex as you that is referred to as **homosexual** and is commonly called being 'gay', which can refer to both men and women, but the formal word for a woman or girl who is attracted to other women/girls is lesbian. Those who are attracted to both sexes are termed **bisexual**, or 'bi', and people who think they may like those of their own gender can refer to themselves as bi-curious. Some people prefer describing themselves as **'queer'**.

LAURA'S Q & A

"I like girls not boys. How can I tell my friends or family?"

Regardless of whether you like girls or boys, dating can be a cause of conflict with your parents. Having relationships with boys or girls may be new, and it could be an adjustment for friends or family to see that you are interested in this – no matter who it is with.

Work out who would be reasonable and positive about this. By speaking to these people first you will get a chance to experiment with talking about yourself in this personal way. Just because your sister/brother/mum/dad/gran react in one way doesn't mean everyone else will, and it is important to have your 'support team' in place if others find it hard to be relaxed about it.

It might feel simpler to imagine telling your friends first. You might find if you have negative reactions it might affect your friendship with the people you have told. This can be difficult but ultimately it isn't good to be around people who cannot accept us as we are. It's more tricky with family as it is likely that you rely on them for your home and care.

This is another reason to think carefully about who in your family you tell, and when. Talk it through with supportive people and bear in mind that if you weren't making a statement about yourself (the fact you like girls), but simply saying you like someone, you probably wouldn't think of making a big announcement. It is important to remember that although you want those close to you to know, there's no rush, telling them now or later won't change your feelings.

BOYS, GIRLS OR NO THANKS?

'I'm attracted to boys and girls, but didn't realise that until I was 18. I thought I was just attracted to guys before that.'

'I was about 12 years old when I started feeling any sort of attraction towards guys but by the time I was 16 I began feeling attracted to girls.'

'Being a teenager, I was expected to have a boyfriend even when I felt confused about my attraction towards girls so when all my friends had boyfriends I felt left out. I also felt conflicted, growing up with Pakistani parents puberty, sex and sexuality are things that should not be discussed.'

LAURA'S Q & A

"There's a boy in my class who I like. My friends asked him out for me and since then I've seen him looking at me but he hasn't said anything. What should I do?"

The fact that he is looking at you suggests that even if he hasn't responded, he certainly heard what your friends were saying.

One possibility is that he might be shy and self-conscious or even under some pressure, and perhaps you are both a bit unsure of what to do next.

→

I wonder if the boot were on the other foot and it had been his friends talking to you, whether you might also have been stuck for an answer. You might have even wondered if they were for real, or if it was all a big joke. That's the problem with getting other people to speak for us. I suspect that as you like him, it may be up to you to make the first move. That doesn't need to mean running over and asking him out, but next time you see him looking, smile at him. If he smiles back, take that as a good sign and try talking to him. Once you have taken the first step to an actual conversation, he or you may feel a little more confident about suggesting meeting up.

Of course, there is also a chance he might not be interested, and when you try to make contact he may not respond in the way that you hope. It can feel painful not to have our feelings returned, but there's nothing you can do about that. We can't control who we are attracted to and sometimes it just doesn't work out.

If you do go on a date together, let yourself have fun and be yourself. You need to get to know each other, and fancying someone across the classroom might change when you get to know them. You might find that you completely fall for him or that time with this boy means that he loses some of his shine for you. You will only find this out through some contact and that will mean that one of you has to risk at least talking to the other!

I don't want to be an interfering mum-type but if you do end up going on a date, you need to be straight with your parents or carers and let them know where you are going. It's just that, as yet, you don't know this boy very well and if you want to cut the date short, you need to be able to get home safely.

CRUSH TO RELATIONSHIP

You know, all these thoughts and feelings don't actually shut down once you hit 18. To be honest, we all have crushes – or are attracted to other people – throughout our lives: we meet new friends and think they are tremendous, we admire celebrities because we like the way they look and even sometimes spend the odd minute dreaming about random people we meet and how our lives might be different if only we knew them better.

There are sometimes very good reasons why crushes should stay in our heads. If, for example, your crush is on a good friend, you may need to think a bit about how they would feel if they knew about it. Would it mean they felt uncomfortable being around you? Friends are important and while you are in the throes of a severe crush it may be hard to remember how much you value the friendship, so do tread carefully.

Say the object of your crush is someone around your age who you know pretty well and you actually have the chance to find out if a real relationship between the two of you would work. That could lead to the two of you going out with each other. You might have already had your first relationship – an understanding with a girl that what you had between you wasn't just friends, or perhaps a boy in your class who asked you out so you became his girlfriend for a while. You may never have even gone on a date or kissed but you just both wanted to make clear that you kind of liked each other. It might be that having this relationship made you feel a bit special in your group. The fact that you might have been one of the first to be in this situation could have meant other people saw you in a different light and you enjoyed that feeling. That's fine, but as you go forwards, getting into romantic relationships should really be about how you feel about the other person – not what your friends think about it. You might struggle with that if you really want to fit in with your group of gal-pals but as I said in the section on friendships, real friends want the best for you and they love you for who you are. Not who you're going out with.

'When I was 16 I started seeing a boy in my class at school and we fell completely in love. He made my skin shiver and this huge smile take over my face. We broke up four years later but I still remember the feeling.'

'I first kissed a boy at junior school when I was 10. We just pressed our lips together and stood behind the classrooms with everyone else because that's what the cool gang did.'

I think I like boys and I might like a boyfriend but the only girls who date at my age are the super popular girls.

Going out with someone can be great. As with your friends, your boyfriend or girlfriend should be someone special who makes you feel good about yourself. Over the course of the next few years you may well get your heart broken, and break a few hearts yourself. That's a subject that could fill a whole other book. For now, though, I just want to say you have your whole life to come. There's no rush. Enjoy who you are and never be with anyone who makes you feel bad about yourself.

'I actually kissed the boy next door when I was about eight (he was the same age), but the first proper adult kiss I had was with my first boyfriend at 13. We held hands, kissed ... then I ran away!'

'When I was 12, I started to have feelings for a close female friend of mine, but I didn't start to recognise that as attraction or a "crush" until a few years later. I didn't know that it was possible for women to be interested in other women in that way, so I found it hard to put a name on what it was that I felt towards her.'

'My first proper kiss was when I was 15. I was worried I wasn't doing it right at first, but afterwards I realised I had nothing to be scared about.

'My first boyfriend was when I was in primary school boy-friend in Year 6. He took me for ice cream.'

'I was 16. He walked me from school to the bus stop and kissed me. I floated home. The next day he handed me a letter. It said he'd decided to go out with Tracey instead.'

'I'm attracted mainly to girls and my first snog was with another girl in the corner of the playground.'

LAURA'S Q & A

"I really like my boyfriend but we've never actually been alone together. I'm worried that when we are he may try and kiss me or something and I don't know what to do."

Before you start wondering about kissing your boyfriend it might be good to get to know him a bit more. That would help you both to work out what your relationship is and what might happen next.

It sounds to me that you're not feeling confident about what's going on and that might mean you don't feel ready for kissing. If that's the case let him know that though you like him, you want to take things slowly.

As with all things that affect us emotionally, it is really important only to do what you feel ready for and not to force something to happen because you think you ought to or because you want to please your boyfriend. Trust your gut and if it is saying 'no' then listen and wait; it won't be long before it's saying 'yes' (even if it's not to this boyfriend).

If, however, your worry is about not knowing what to do (but want to kiss him), then that is a different matter! I remember when I was at school some of the girls snogged their pillows in the way they'd seen people kissing on the TV to try and learn the technique. I tried this and just got a face full of pillow! You won't know what it's like until you are actually kissing someone and then you'll find that you can just do it. Take your time and don't be afraid to stop if you feel it is going too fast.

How you feel now doesn't have to set in stone who you are going to be later on in your life (and that's not to say that what you're feeling at this moment won't seem immensely important to you). Remember, though, this is your time to try things out in your head. You don't have to act on these thoughts or feelings and there's no law about how you should feel or think. If your crush is for your best girl pal and you catch yourself wondering what it may be like to kiss her, that's OK. The same is true as if your crush is for the boy in your class that up until five minutes ago was a real pain in the backside because he was always teasing you.

As well as getting to know your changing body, this is a time to get to know your own mind. Later in life, when relationships start to involve serious commitments like living together or even starting a family, it's good to have a firm idea about who and what sort of person you are attracted to.

'My first kiss was at 18 and was followed rapidly by a second kiss. It took me a long while to get one; I wasn't stopping there.'

'My first proper kiss was in secondary with my first "boyfriend" in Year 8. It was absolutely rubbish! We had built up to it for so long (and I carried mints around with me just in case!) and then it was just rubbish.'

'I felt disappointed my first kiss wasn't like how it is portrayed in the media.'

'My first boyfriend was a guy called Andrew when I was 14. We went to the movies and we kissed for the entire film, like two hours. Honestly, it was too much but I wasn't sure how to ask him to stop.'

> *I have a boy crush and I know I also fancy girls, but I haven't told my parents - I don't know how!*

> *I have a boyfriend and he's very nice. Since I hit puberty I have been immersed in boys and I have kissed one or two.*

There's absolutely nothing wrong with 'crushing' on anyone. However, if you have a crush on an older person you have to know that this will never be able to become a real relationship. There are strict laws in this country that absolutely forbid anyone over the age of 16 from having a sexual relationship with a 'minor' (that's someone under 16). Even if you feel like you are very mature, even if you know that you'd really get on well if you were together in real life. It is way more complicated than you are able to imagine, I promise. Keep it as a daydream, as a fantasy – there's no harm in that. If, however, they show any signs of feeling things for you, massive warning bells should be going off in your head. This is not cool. This is not a reflection on you – it doesn't mean you are so amazing that this older person can see past your age and appreciate the wonderful you inside. It means that this person is not quite right because they should know better. They are the adult – the power lies with them. If they think it's a good idea to be in a relationship with a child (and if you're under 16 you are a child in the eyes of the law) no matter how special, or sophisticated or desirable that child is – that person is not safe to be around and you'd best steer clear.

Part 3
SEX: ONE WORD, MANY MEANINGS

Sex. Oh my, there's a lot that little word covers, isn't there? On the one hand, it is a word that describes an act when two people have sexual intercourse. On the other hand, it can describe your gender. As I only have two hands, I'm going to have to borrow some more because I haven't even started on 'sexy', and what that's all about, so it's no surprise if you find it all a bit confusing.

'Sexy' is a word I'll bet you've heard a lot, and from when you were really pretty tiny. You might have heard someone described as sexy, I'm sure you've heard it in a million song lyrics, you may joke with your friends about looking sexy or even acting sexy you might even have someone in your life who when you think about them it feels sort of… sexy.

ACTUALLY HAVING SEX

Let's start with sexual intercourse. This is pretty simple. It's when two people get their genitals together and penetration occurs (one person enters the other person). When a man and a woman have sex, the man's penis becomes erect (this is because loads of blood in his body all charges to his penis, which makes it stiff – don't worry, it's not as dramatic as that sounds; he still has plenty of blood to keep him going). The man puts his erect penis inside the woman's vaginal opening. Some thrusting takes place and (usually) finishes when the man ejaculates by having an orgasm. When this happens, semen (a liquid which contains sperm – think man-tadpoles – and is created in his scrotum or balls) shoots out from the tip of his penis. Once inside a woman's body, sperm can travel to the ovaries and may fertilise an egg (which is the start of making a baby).

That said, men and women can and do have sexual intercourse without making babies. The sperm won't find an egg every time although it could, in theory, unless contraception is being used. Contraception is what we call the various ways to deliberately stop the sperm meeting the egg. There are different types of contraception available including pills that the woman takes, or a special cover (called a condom) that a man can put on his willy to stop the sperm getting into the woman's body.

You may hear rumours about women who got pregnant from sitting on a toilet seat after a man had been to the loo – this is not true. It can't happen. You might have heard tales about some woman and a man who didn't have full-on sex but just messed around a bit (they were touching each other's bits) and the man had an orgasm (or 'came' as it is often called) near the woman's vagina and she got pregnant. In theory, this one could happen. It's quite unlikely, but because the sperm are contained in a liquid (semen) it helps them get to places, so if a man ejaculates near the vaginal opening even if he hasn't been inside, it could travel up through the vagina to the ovaries to meet an egg. Other people may say things like you can't get pregnant unless you are lying down, or you can't get pregnant the first time you have sex or even you can't get pregnant if you have your period. You can. The only way that a woman can't get pregnant is if she uses contraception or her partner does.

ORGASMS

Okey dokey. So, that is sex, that's what all the fuss is about. However, it doesn't really answer all the questions does it? It doesn't really explain why people go on about it so much, about why it's so important and really, if you think about it, it doesn't really explain why on earth anyone would want to do it, unless they actually wanted a baby.

Penetration, or sexual intercourse, as I've described it above, is only one aspect of the whole thing. And if you think about it, if that was all that there was to it, what would same-sex couples get up to? For a start, having an orgasm or 'coming' isn't just for boys. The way in which the female body reaches orgasm is different from how it is for boys. Girls don't usually produce a liquid (ejaculate) when they reach orgasm, but instead experience a really nice feeling which floods through their whole body. There are lots of ways in which adults can be close to each other and make each other feel nice or have orgasms that doesn't involve sexual intercourse.

FEELING SEXY

So, let's leave that there for a bit and go back to sexy. If your best friend tells you she thinks that a boy from another class is sexy, does that mean she wants to have sex with him? If you and your mates joke about looking sexy in a bikini, does that mean you all want to have sex with any random boy walking past? That sounds really daft, I know, but isn't sexy about having sex? Well, no. Not necessarily. You've probably talked about fancying people boys, girls, celebrities, whatever and we know fancying someone is pretty different from liking them as a friend (more on this in Boys, Girls or No Thanks on page 166). I guess fancying someone is the start of sexy. It means you are drawn to them, and probably want to be close to them in a physical way.

When people talk about looking sexy, it often means that there is something about that person's appearance that makes them seem desirable in a way that isn't about being mates. That could be something about their looks, a way they have about them, it could even be what they are wearing, or just the fact they make you laugh. When you fancy someone, it is about wanting to be more than just friends. That's the first bit. When you talk about 'sexy', you're talking about that 'more than friends' thing becoming physical. That usually starts with holding hands, or putting arms around each other. Or, even, a kiss.

'I was 15 and we kissed at a house party. He said I tasted delicious (I'd just eaten some Skittles).'

'I went for a walk with a friend and he gave me a wet sloppy kiss which was pretty disgusting.'

Plus, let's get real – it can be fun giggling about sex and being sexy. Everyone does (yes, even grown-ups). Sometimes we giggle about stuff because it feels a bit personal, and that can be embarrassing, so we laugh. Sometimes it can be just plain funny. By all means enjoy having a laugh with your pals, dreaming about your true love with your best mate, or just ignoring the whole thing until you feel ready.

There's so much chatter about sex and sexy things. As you get older – or maybe even now – you'll hear boys bleating on about sex and it can seem as if the whole event has been designed just for them. That is just not true. (See page 76, and the box on Women and Sexuality.) Women can and do enjoy sex and you should never think of it as a favour you are doing for someone. When you are old enough and ready, the only reason you should have sex is because you want to and you enjoy it.

You may have heard people talking about losing their virginity and wondered what that means? Or perhaps your mates have been discussing who is and who isn't a virgin. A virgin is someone who hasn't had sex, so losing your virginity is a way of describing the first time you've had sex. That's it. There's no added hidden meaning there. Sometimes people will call someone a virgin in a nasty way, as if to say there is something wrong with them. That's just not true. There's nothing wrong with not having sex with someone; even once you are over 16 having sex with someone should be your choice and your choice only. Your body, your choice, and your business.

THE AGE OF CONSENT

The more you hear about sex, the more you talk about it with friends, or see stuff on telly, music videos, or movies, the more interested you'll get. Of course, at some stage you'll want to experiment. It's really natural to want more but – and this is the most important thing I can say – do remember this: the law of this country is that girls and boys must not have sex until they are 16. This is known as the age of consent. The idea is that the average boy or girl who is younger than 16 will not be ready for the emotional consequences of sex. Letting someone get that close to you is a massively big deal. Don't even think about doing it to make someone like you, don't even think about doing it to look good in front of your mates and don't even think about doing it until you are good and ready and know you can really trust the person you are with. Seriously. And, when I say it is against the law I mean that you or the person you are with (especially if they are over 16) can get into serious trouble with life-long consequences. Plenty of people don't have sex until they are much older than 16 – late teens/early 20s (and some may be older still!). In some cultures or religions and/or according to some people's personal belief systems, couples should not have sex unless they are married.

LAURA'S Q & A

"I've been with my boyfriend for almost three months but I know we'll be together forever. We're both 13 and I really love him. I love kissing him so does that mean I'm ready to have sex?"

It is lovely to meet someone, and I reckon when you kiss you're having all sorts of feelings in your body. Because that's nice (and exciting!), it might feel really urgent to go further with him. Plus, you may not have had these feelings before, so they are new and you're not sure if having them is a sign you should go all the way.

Having sex is a big deal and has consequences. You might think it's just going on a bit from kissing, but it is more. (That's why there is a legal age of consent.) Our bodies develop much faster than our emotions and we all spend most of our first 20 years catching up with our physical selves. If you have sex with your boyfriend, even if you avoid pregnancy and get away with breaking the law, your relationship won't be the same. Our first experiences will hopefully ⟶

leave us with good memories, but could result in confusion and regret. I understand that three months can feel like a long time when you are 13, but it is still not so long in terms of your whole life.

I wonder if you are contacting me because even though a bit of you is very excited, another bit isn't sure. You might feel like you need to please your boyfriend or be concerned that he'll split up with you. I don't know him so I can't say what he may or may not do, but if you do stay with him forever that's a long time. It means you don't need to worry about having sex now because you'll have years ahead of you.

REALLY IMPORTANT!!!

If you've spoken about sex at school you've probably talked about boundaries. Boundaries are like lines that you put around something to stop anyone or everyone barging around where they are not wanted. It's really important to have some boundaries around your body, too.

If anyone is talking to you, or looking at you, in a way that makes you feel uncomfortable, they are invading your boundaries. Whether it is someone your age, older, or an adult, tell them to stop. If that doesn't work, tell someone else. This is a big deal and needs to be handled quickly and firmly. Choose who to tell – it doesn't have to be a parent or carer; it could be another family member, a teacher, a club leader or any other grown-up in your life that you know in your heart you can trust, and you know in your heart will always put you first. Please do this, please. You've done absolutely nothing wrong, even if you've played along a bit because it started off as fun.

LAURA'S Q & A

"There's a man who lives on my street who looks at me and my friends in a way that makes us feel a bit uncomfortable. If we're wearing skirts he jokes about us having nice legs. I don't want to get anyone into trouble but I just don't know what to do."

Unwanted attention – even jokes or compliments – can leave us feeling exposed, really uncomfortable and even a bit powerless and that isn't right, so good on you for speaking out. He could be saying this to other girls as well, who also feel uncomfortable but haven't felt able to ask for help.

Any adult should know not to make jokes and say personal things like that to a child.

Your gut is telling you something is wrong, that's a great sign that you are aware of your feelings. Nobody should be allowed to make you feel like this and it's important that you talk to an adult about this situation; don't be afraid to speak up.

Sometimes it can be people nearer your own age who can make you feel this way if they are making jokes or other comments about your body. The thing to remember is that if somebody is making you feel uncomfortable it is wrong, and you don't have to put up with it. Find the adult in your life that you know you can trust and ask for their help.

Part 4
LAST THOUGHTS

You've doubtless heard people say that these years are the 'best' of your life. I clearly remember being told this, and the problem with hearing it constantly is that, in those times when you're finding life a bit of a struggle, it can make you wonder if you're doing something wrong.

I think what it really means is that this is your time. Yours to explore the world, to explore yourself. Try things out for size – whether that's blue hair or being obsessed with history, or rocks and crystals, or training at a gym, or fighting for your rights, or becoming an inventor or a business genius, or being with girls, or being with boys, or starting your own channel or getting into a lab, or even writing a book of your own.

Just don't let anyone, ever, say 'that's not for girls'. If you're interested in something, and you want to try it out, do. Your time.

However, that's not to say that you won't feel some real pressures during these years. And that, coupled with the fact that the amount of control you have over your life is still fairly limited, can sometimes feel massively frustrating.

Each of us is different and you could be feeling a billion things in any given second (and then a whole billion more the next second). Some of the great girls who spoke to me while I was writing this book told me what they felt about growing up – perhaps some of their thoughts may ring true for you?

How about you?
What do you make of it all?
Fill in your ideas on the following page.

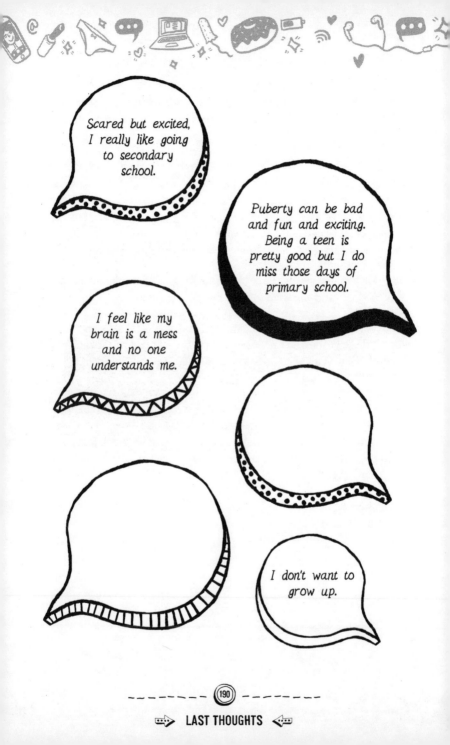

LAST THOUGHTS

That's pretty much it but I want to leave you with some more wise words from the women who've been through it. (I really enjoyed reading these, and I hope you will, too).

Good luck, and we all hope that you have got something from reading this book. And, most importantly, we wish you all the best with coming through puberty, growing up and moving on in your lives.

'Being a teenager was all at the same time brilliant and boring and horrible and painful and confusing and just plain crazy! You could have a completely normal day and feel like the world had changed, or have a completely brilliant day and feel like crying all night.'

'It was hard up till about 16, I was shy, awkward, didn't think I looked that good. It was a time when I didn't really know who I was; I spent a lot of time at a friends' houses as home was a bit stormy at times - me and my mum clashed big time and I just wanted to get away and enjoy myself.'

'It was wonderful, terrible, hideous, tedious and very exciting. I swung between being exceptionally confident and happy to loathing myself. But it was much better than that bit between ages 7-11. 10-year-old girls and boys can be very horrible.'

'It was fun. But there was a time when I first went to secondary school that I was so down all the time and felt extremely alone. I also fought a lot with my mum which I really regret now as it must have been a really rubbish time for her.'

'Being a teenager was a real mix of highs and lows. Lots of anxieties and insecurities and keeping secrets from my parents but always colourful and a bit chaotic.'

'My mother never appreciated that I was a completely different person to her and never stopped projecting her dreams and ambitions onto me this was particularly difficult as a teenager while I was still living at home.'

'My teenage years were a whirlwind. Brilliant, horrible, frustrating, freeing, happy, sad. I wrote a journal and reading back I had a lot of sadness in me but I was always known as the happy one.'

'It was a combination of fabulous and awful. I was chubby and a bit spotty, but loved making people laugh and was popular as a result.'

'Being a teenager is incredibly exciting because you get to experience so many things for the first time. But it's also very dramatic, as no one is good at being a grown-up yet and everyone makes loads of mistakes.'

'I'm glad I went through my teens when I did because nowadays there is a lot of pressure on young people to "fit in" publicly due to the falseness of social media life. I'm happy to have been around when IRL was the only life.'

'I wish sometimes I could go back to my teenage self and reassure her that everything will turn out OK in the end.'

'It was quite a confusing time. I wish that I had slowed down a bit and enjoyed it and not worried about every last thing quite so much.'

'Although I had friends and loving parents I had no idea who I was and lacked self-confidence. I was also mean to my mum who is now my best friend in the world.'

'Being a teenager was difficult. I was always falling in and out of love and being dumped.'

'It was a very weird time, but if you remember to allow yourself those feelings, and that you're not alone in feeling them, and try to laugh at yourself a little bit, you'll come out the other side feeling amazing.'

And finally? My own personal favourite saying: 'This, too, will pass.'

Lots of love, xxx

FURTHER READING

There are loads of great books, sites and channels out there packed with helpful advice. Here are just a few we like:

PUBERTY INFO

'4 U Growing up – what's it all about?', puberty document NHS choices:

www.nhs.uk/Livewell/puberty/
Documents/4youmarch2010nonprinting.pdf

Handy pdf booklet with lots of factual information about puberty for girls and boys.

GENERAL HELP AND ADVICE

Kidscape (Preventing bullying, protecting children):

www.kidscape.org.uk

A fantastic site dedicated to helping with issues surrounding friendships, loneliness and bullying – from online to real life, including a great section on 'frenemies' and how to move on from friendships that don't make you feel good about yourself.

Childline:

www.childline.org.uk

Packed with advice, games and quizzes, but with good information on puberty and a really serious message of help and support for any child who is feeling unhappy for any reason. There's a free helpline to talk to someone in confidence and advice and message boards on a really wide variety of topics.

SEX/GENDER/SEXUALITY INFO

Brook.org.uk:

www.brook.org.uk

Not specifically designed for kids, but for under-25s. This site has information on all aspects of sexual health and well-being (including abuse, online safety and questions surrounding gender and sexuality).

ONLINE SAFETY

Thinkuknow UK:

www.thinkuknow.co.uk

This site is all about online safety. It is divided into different sections according to age and is run by CEOP (Child Exploitation and Online Protection). It's really user-friendly and full of great advice about staying safe online and what to do if things go wrong.

DIFFICULT FEELINGS

Young minds (Child and adolescent mental health):

www.youngminds.org.uk

This is the absolute go-to site if you want some help, advice or support with anything that may be affecting your mental health. From bullying, self-harm and anxiety, to abuse and eating disorders, they have it covered and can really help.

'Mighty Moe', an anxiety booklet for children:

www.cw.bc.ca/library/pdf/pamphlets/Mighty%20Moe1.pdf

A pdf cartoon booklet all about anxiety with lots of practical tips and advice, plus a story about Mighty Moe who learns to deal with his 'big' feelings. It's a bit 'kiddy' but it's really sound.

DEALING WITH DEATH

Child Bereavement UK:

https://childbereavementuk.org/

This site has help and advice if someone you love has died. It tries to answer questions you may have and also has a helpline so you can talk to someone in complete confidence, plus an app to download to give you support.

YOUNG CARERS

Makewaves (Young carers in focus):

www.makewav.es/ycif

If you're in a position where you are a carer for someone, this site has loads of information and resources to try and help lighten the load. It also contains information about events and support groups for young carers.

SOME COOL SITES TO SEARCH OUT

Shape your culture:

www.shapeyourculture.org.uk

This cracker of a site is run by an organisation called AnyBody UK. It's full of really empowering messages, interviews and news of events. It's really creative and a great place to have a browse.

Betty.me:

https://betty.me

With sections on body, life, people, stuff and style, this is a great website celebrating all things 'girl' with positive messages and plenty of quizzes.

BBC Bitesize:

www.bbc.co.uk/education

You've probably seen these in school and might not want to be spending your free time searching these up, but if you follow the links through for your Keystage, the PHSE and Citizenship subject areas have quite a few interesting and informative little films and clips on a whole variety of subjects from puberty to mental health, relationships, diversity and identity.

'Not your mum', YouTube:

https://www.youtube.com/notyourmum

This channel covers all life advice for girls aged 11 and up. Two women chatting about all the really personal stuff we may wonder about – or worry about and being frank and funny with it.

A mighty girl:

www.amightygirl.com

This features blog posts on subjects ranging from managing money to handling siblings, plus there are great tips on films to watch and books to read, and a great link to set up your own book club.

WORTH A READ

You may be too old for the glorious girls that are Pippi Longstocking or Matilda, or perhaps even the magical worlds of Chris Riddell's *Goth Girl* or Katherine Rundell's *Rooftoppers*, but you've probably seen or read at least one book by Jacqueline Wilson – she writes fantastic and really gripping stories about girls in all sorts of situations. I am too old to have read her books as a girl, but I did read a lot of books by Judy Blume when I was younger. Yes, they're set in America and were written last century, but there is nothing this lady doesn't know about growing up great (start off with *Are you there God? It's me, Margaret* – you won't regret it!)

Another oldie but goodie is the classic *Anne of Green Gables*. Actually, there are six books about the hero, Anne Shirley, who is 11 when the stories start and in her 40s by the end of the series.

His Dark Materials, Philip Pullman and *The Hunger Games*, Suzanne Collins are a bit more up to date and both feature strong female leads: Lyra and Katniss. Of course, Hermione Granger in the Harry Potter books, by J.K. Rowling is pretty unbeatable when it comes to role models.

If you prefer less wizarding and fantasy, the *Ruby Redfort* books by Lauren Child feature 13-year-old Ruby who starts the series as a normal, snarky, teenager and goes on to become a code-cracking ace detective. Or, *Murder Most Unladylike* by Robin Stevens combines the delights of a boarding school with a secret girls-only detective agency.

For some real-life inspiration, *The Diary of Anne Frank* and *I Am Malala*, by Malala Yousafzai, are must-reads.

If women and girls throughout history are your thing, *My Story* (published by Scholastic) is a series of books written like diaries all from the point of view of women or girls – from Queen Victoria or a suffragette to a mill girl or a slave. They're absorbing reads that make a really strong point about what girls can do and be.

Inspiring non-fiction reads include *Goodnight Stories for Rebel Girls* by Elena Favilli and Francesca Cavallo and *Girls are Best* by Sandi Toksvig – both highlight the great women and girls throughout history and are also cracking reads. Also, *Girls Think of Everything* by Catherine Thimmesh – collected tales of women inventors. Did you know that windscreen wipers were invented by a woman?

Now we know there are more sites out there worth visiting, and more fantastic and engaging books to be read. We've listed the ones that we thought were helpful or interesting, but obviously, this list is influenced by our tastes and preferences.

You could use the next couple of pages to write down your own favourites, or perhaps make a note of any recommendations you get from other people, whether it's a book your friend has read and has said you've just *got* to read next, or something that's been suggested by someone at school. Making a note of them means you've got a handy reference guide all of your own.

. . . .

. . . .

. . . .

. . . .

. . . .

. . . .

. . . .

. . . .

. . . .

. . . .

. . . .

NOTES

NOTES

....
....
....
....
....
....
....
....
....
....
....
....
....
....

ACKNOWLEDGEMENTS

SOPHIE

This book wouldn't have been written without my own great girl: Ruby. She is the apple of my eye and has taught me more than I could have imagined; it is nothing but a privilege to be her mother. My husband, Paul, walks by my side – even when I fall behind. It is his hand I hold.

The other person who made this happen is Charlotte at Bloomsbury, and I must thank Sarah and the whole team for their support and hard work. Thanks, too, to Flo who divined the fuzzy images in my head and brought them to life.

I have learned a lot throughout this whole process, and will particularly cherish the many conversations with Lozzie when I actually thought I'd pee myself laughing.

I want to acknowledge the wonderful women and great girls who allowed me to use their words. It wouldn't be the same without their 'Wise Words' and 'Girl Quotes'. I'm also endlessly grateful to the women and their daughters – those I know and some who I never met – who took time to read through sections and get back to me with their comments and advice. Special mention to Harriet Y, and also to Jess D.

There's another group of people I want to acknowledge: the mums. My 'unassailable' mother, Judy, comes first but growing up I was lucky enough to have great friends with 'cool mums' – in particular Rose, mother to my own BFF Kesia, and also the sublime Jude, both of whom introduced me to worlds beyond my own…

Finally, no one was more surprised than me to have early support from Sarah Brown. Please visit theirworld.org to learn more about her important work.

LAURA

Thank you to all the women and men who move through our lives and let us grow to be the most of ourselves we can be. Thank you to those women who offered their interest, wisdom and time to this book, you know who you are. Love and respect to my Mum and Dad and my fantastic husband Nathan whose love and support make so much possible. Most of all I want to thank our inspiring, lively, funny, creative growing-up-great girls Sylvie and Nancy. I wouldn't have done this without you.

MADDY

To my inspiring and amazing daughter, Asha, with love.

FLO

Big up to my agent Karolina for making me feel like an adult. Thank you to everyone at BuzzFeed who encouraged me to draw. Thank you to Jim for always loading the dishwasher so nicely, Hannah J for being my inspiration, and Jo for being like my right arm, and a couple of minor organs too. Thank you Lauren for being my gal pal forever, love you. And thank you Mum and Dad for not being visibly disappointed when I gave up being a scientist.

INDEX